OPUS DEI

THE TRUTH BEHIND THE MYTH

AVE MARIA.

Je vous salue, Marie,

Pleine de grâce,

Le Seigneur est avec vous, vous êtes
bénie par dessus toutes les femmes,

Et Jésus le fruit de vos entrailles
est béni.

Sainte Marie, Mère de Dieu, priez pour nous, pauvres
pécheurs, maintenant et à l'heure de notre mort.
Ainsi soit-il.

OPUS DEI

THE TRUTH BEHIND THE MYTH

Exploring the mysteries of one of the most controversial and
powerful forces in world religion, from its humble beginnings to its
great prominence and influence across five continents today

Maggy Whitehouse

HERMES
HOUSE

This edition is published by Hermes House

Hermes House is an imprint of Anness Publishing Ltd
Hermes House, 88–89 Blackfriars Road,
London SE1 8HA

tel. 020 7401 2077; fax 020 7633 9499; www.annesspublishing.com

Anness Publishing has a new picture agency outlet for images for
publishing, promotions or advertising. Please visit our website
www.practicalpictures.com for more information.

A CIP catalogue record for this book is available from the
British Library.

Designed and produced for Anness Publishing by
THE BRIDGEWATER BOOK COMPANY LTD.

Publisher Joanna Lorenz
Editorial Director Helen Sudell
Art Director Michael Whitehead
Production Controller Wendy Lawson

ETHICAL TRADING POLICY
At Anness Publishing we believe that business should be conducted in
an ethical and ecologically sustainable way, with respect for the
environment and a proper regard to the replacement of the natural
resources we employ.

As a publisher, we use a lot of wood pulp to make high-quality paper
for printing, and that wood commonly comes from spruce trees. We are
therefore currently growing more than 500,000 trees in two Scottish
forest plantations near Aberdeen – Berrymoss (130 hectares/320 acres)
and West Touxhill (125 hectares/305 acres). The forests we manage
contain twice the number of trees employed each year in paper-making
for our books.

Because of this ongoing ecological investment programme, you, as our
customer, can have the pleasure and reassurance of knowing that a tree is
being cultivated on your behalf to naturally replace the materials used to
make the book you are holding.

Our forestry programme is run in accordance with the UK Woodland
Assurance Scheme (UKWAS) and will be certified by the internationally
recognized Forest Stewardship Council (FSC). The FSC is a non-
government organization dedicated to promoting responsible
management of the world's forests. Certification ensures forests are
managed in an environmentally sustainable and socially responsible basis.
For further information about this scheme, go to
www.annesspublishing.com/trees

1 0 9 8 7 6 5 4 3 2 1

PICTURE ACKNOWLEGEMENTS
Anness Publishing would like to thank the following for kindly supplying
photographs for this book: 1 Getty Images; 2 Bridgeman Art Library; 3 Opus Dei
UK Information Office (ODuk); 4 ODuk; 5 bl ODuk, bc AKG-images, br ODuk;
6-7 Corbis; 8 tl iStock photography, bl Photos.com; 9 tr iStock photography, cr
AKG-images; 10 tr iStock photography, bl Corbis; 11 tl Corbis, cr Photos.com, br
Corbis; 12 tr Photos.com, bl Corbis; 13 tr Corbis, br Corbis; 14 tr Corbis, bl
Corbis; 15 tr Bridgeman Art Library, br Corbis; 16 tl Corbis, br Corbis; 17 tr
Corbis, tl Corbis, br Picture Desk; 18 cl Picture Desk, br Picture Desk; 19 tl
Corbis, br Corbis; 20-21 ODuk; 22 tl ODuk, br ODuk; 23 tr ODuk, cl ODuk,
br ODuk; 24 tr ODuk, bl ODuk; 25 tr ODuk, br ODuk; 26 tr Bridgeman Art
Library, bl AKG-images; 27 tl ODuk, cr ODuk, br ODuk; 28 tr Corbis, bl Corbis;
29 tr Corbis, cr Corbis; 30 tl ODuk, bl ODuk; 31 tl ODuk, br ODuk; 32 tr
ODuk, bl ODuk; 33 tl ODuk, tr ODuk, br Corbis; 34 tl ODuk; 35 tr ODuk, bl
Corbis, cr Corbis; 36-37 Picture Desk; 38 tr ODuk, bl ODuk; 39 tr Corbis, br
ODuk; 40 tr Erika Larsen@reduxpictures, bl ODuk; 41 tr ODuk, br ODuk; 42 tl
iStock photography, br iStock photography; 43 tl Corbis, cr iStock photography;
44 tl Picture Desk, br Corbis; 45 tr Corbis, cr Corbis; 46 tr ODuk, bl ODuk; 47
tr ODuk, bl Yuri Goul@Annomedia; 48 bl ODuk, tr Erika Larsen@reduxpictures;
49 tr Erika Larsen@reduxpictures, br AKG-images; 50 tr Erika
Larsen@reduxpictures, bl iStock photography; 51 tl Bridgeman Art Library, br
Erika Larsen@reduxpictures; 52 tl iStock photography, br Picture Desk; 53 tl
iStock photography, tr Corbis, br Picture Desk; 54 tr ODuk, bl Corbis; 55 tr Erika
Larsen, bl AKG-images; 56 tr Corbis, bl Jonathan Bailey; 57 tl Corbis, br Picture
Desk; 58 tr Corbis, bl ODuk; 59 tr ODuk, bl ODuk; 60 tr ODuk, bl ODuk; 61
tr ODuk, cr ODuk, bl iStock photography; 62 tr iStock photography, bl Corbis;
63 tr Corbis, br Corbis; 64-65 Erika Larsen@reduxpictures; 66 tr ODuk, bl
ODuk; 67 tr ODuk, br iStock photo-graphy; 68 tr ODuk, bl ODuk; 69 tl ODuk,
cr ODuk, br ODuk; 70 bl Sarah Feinstein; 71 tr Sarah Feinstein, cr Getty Images; 72
tr OKuk, cr ODuk, bl ODuk; 73 tr ODuk, br iStock photography; 74 tr ODuk, bl
ODuk; 75 tr ODuk, cr ODuk; 76-77 Getty Images; 78 tr iStock photography, bl
Corbis; 79 tr Corbis, br Picture Desk; 80 tl Picture Desk, br Empic; 81 tr iStock
photography, br iStockphotography; 82 tl Corbis, br Corbis; 83 tl Picture Desk, cr
ODuk; 84 tr Corbis, bl Corbis; 85 tl Corbis, cr iStock photography; 86 tl ODuk;
87 tr ODuk, bl ODuk; 88 tr Empic, bl ODuk,bc ODuk; 89 tl Empic, br Corbis;
90 tl Empic; 91 tr Empic, br ODuk; 92 tc Erika Larsen@reduxpictures, bl iStock
photography; 93 cr ODuk; 94 tr Corbis, bl Corbis; 95 br ODuk; 96 tr Picture
Desk, bl ODuk.

Every effort has been made to obtain permission to reproduce copyright material,
but there may be cases where we have been unable to trace a copyright holder.
The publisher will be happy to correct any omissions in future printings.

Images are listed in clockwise order from the top (t = top, c = centre, b = bottom,
r = right, l = left, tr = top right etc.).

CONTENTS

PART ONE

THE CATHOLIC CHURCH

It would be impossible to understand Opus Dei without first examining its foundation, the Roman Catholic Church. The Church believes that God incarnated in the world through his son, Jesus Christ, who was crucified and was resurrected from the dead. These beliefs are written down in the New Testament and were formulated in the ancient creeds of the Ecumenical Councils of Nicaea in the year AD325 and Constantinople in AD381. In addition, the Church believes in the Virgin Birth, obedience to the pope, and the sanctity of life. The Mass, or Holy Eucharist, is the central pillar of the Catholic faith and there are seven holy sacraments. Catholicism disallows women priests, divorce, contraception and abortion. All these views and practices are also fundamental to the life of every member of Opus Dei.

RIGHT Ecclesiastical procession in St Peter's Basilica, Vatican City, Rome. It is considered to be the holiest church in Christianity and can seat 60,000 people.

CATHOLIC BELIEF

IN THE NEW TESTAMENT, JESUS ASSIGNED THE RESPONSIBILITY OF ESTABLISHING THE CHURCH TO HIS DISCIPLE PETER. ACCORDING TO LEGEND, PETER WENT TO ROME, WHERE HE BECAME THE FIRST POPE. AFTER HIS DEATH, HIS WORK WAS CARRIED ON BY A SUCCESSION OF CHRISTIAN LEADERS WHO WERE LATER RETROSPECTIVELY CALLED "POPES" BY THE CHURCH. JESUS' APOSTLES APPROVED OFFICIAL TEACHERS WHO BECAME KNOWN AS "BISHOPS". THEY ORDAINED THE NEXT GENERATION OF BISHOPS. THIS CONTINUOUS LINE OF ORDINATION, KNOWN AS THE "APOSTOLIC SUCCESSION", HAS CONTINUED TO THE PRESENT DAY.

ABOVE Jesus Christ's crucifixion is depicted in every Catholic Church worldwide. Believers often wear an individual crucifix to remind them of Christ's suffering for the redemption of mankind.

ABOVE Diagram of the Holy Trinity, God the Father, God the Son and God the Holy Spirit, to explain the transcendent mystery of three separate aspects of divinity simultaneously forming one God.

RIGHT According to Catholic doctrine, Jesus' mother, Mary, conceived her son through the Holy Spirit and remained a virgin for life. The story of the Nativity is told in the gospels of Matthew and Luke.

The Roman empire legally recognized Christianity in AD313 and, in AD380, it became the official religion of the Roman empire. Over the centuries many divisions occurred within the Christian faith, ultimately forming alternative beliefs including Protestant, Lutheran, Methodist, Baptist, Pentecostalist, and Greek and Russian Orthodox, but for the first 1,000 years after the death of Christ, all of Christianity was Catholic.

In history, the Catholic Church is remembered for good works, including education, and for its saints. It is also known for the Spanish Inquisition,

which killed thousands of unbelievers over a period of just 14 years and continued to seek out heresy for a further 400 years in the belief that people's souls would be saved if they recanted from heresy and turned to Christ.

THE PROTESTANT REFORMATION

The Reformation, which divided the Christian Church into Catholic and Protestant, began on 31 October 1517, when a German monk, Martin Luther, nailed his 95 theses to the Castle Church door in Wittenberg, Germany. The documents included an attack on the pope and on the sale of Indulgences — the giving of alms or services to the Church in return for partial forgiveness of sins by Church officials. Luther taught the doctrine of justification by faith: that salvation is a gift of God's grace, through Christ, to all who believe. He also translated the Bible from Greek and Hebrew into German. All the countries of Europe followed his example by translating the Scriptures into their own languages.

King Henry VIII of England was to become one of the most powerful instruments of the Reformation — even though he had been granted the title "defender of the Faith" by the pope for his pro-Catholic views. Henry and his wife, Catherine of Aragon, had no sons but one daughter, which, in those times, was regarded as the equivalent to being childless. When the King fell in love with Anne Boleyn, who had Protestant leanings, he began to investigate the possibility of annulling his marriage to Catherine. This was opposed by Catholic Europe and the pope. Consequently, Henry decided to break away from the Catholic Church in order to marry Anne and hopefully have a male heir.

However, Queen Anne also only produced a daughter and she was accused of adultery and treason and executed. It was Anne's daughter, Queen Elizabeth I, who defied Catholic Spain and France and established the Protestant religion in England from that time onward. Catholicism became marginalized in Britain and, in 1701, the Act of Settlement was passed to ensure that the British throne went only to Protestant heirs.

THE CHURCH TODAY

The Catholic Church is still the largest branch of Christianity in the world, with more than one billion baptized members, 50 per cent of whom live in the Americas and 25 per cent of whom are in Europe. The current views of the Roman Catholic Church concerning other belief systems were documented in a Vatican declaration *Dominus Iesus*, by Pope John Paul II, in September 2000, which reaffirms that salvation is available only through Jesus Christ and that religions other than Christianity are "gravely deficient". This is despite the fact that the Second Vatican Council in the 1960s issued a Declaration on other faiths saying: "The Catholic Church rejects nothing of what is true and holy in these religions. She has a high regard for the manner of life and conduct, the precepts and teachings, which, although differing ... nonetheless often reflect a ray of that truth which enlightens all men."

THE HOLY TRINITY

The concept of the Holy Trinity is central to the doctrine of the Roman Catholic faith. It states that in the unity of God there are three persons:

ABOVE Castle Church, Wittenberg in Germany, as it is today. It was on the doors of this church that Martin Luther nailed his 95 theses against the Catholic Church and inspired the Reformation, which was to divide Christianity into two separate belief systems.

LEFT Martin Luther nailing his 95 theses on to the Castle Church door. Luther was a monk and his marriage to Katharina von Bora in 1525 reintroduced the practice of clerical marriage to the Christian tradition.

the Father, the Son, and the Holy Spirit. These three are distinct from each other as well as being one. This concept is perhaps best defined in the words of the creed attributed to the 4th-century Archbishop of Alexandria, St Athanasius: "The Father is God, the Son is God, and the Holy Spirit is God, and yet there are not three Gods but one God." In the Trinity, the Son is begotten of the Father and the Holy Spirit proceeds from both the Father and the Son. This, the Church teaches, is the revelation regarding God's nature that Jesus, the Son of God, came to deliver to the world.

ST PAUL AND WOMEN

Although the Catholic Church is descended from St Peter, it follows St Paul's teachings on many subjects, including the role of women. St Paul in the New Testament makes it clear that although a woman could pray or prophesy in a church, she was not permitted to teach or have authority over a man, or to challenge the teaching of a priest. The Early Church Fathers confirmed Paul's views on women and the priesthood, and this tradition continues. In 1994, Pope John Paul II formally declared that the Church does not have the power to ordain women. They can, however, enter holy orders as nuns.

THE SEVEN SACRAMENTS

CATHOLIC LIFE IS DEFINED BY THE SEVEN SACRAMENTS, WHICH ARE CONSIDERED OUTWARD AND VISIBLE SIGNS OF GOD'S INNER, INVISIBLE GRACE. THEY ARE: BAPTISM, CONFESSION, THE HOLY EUCHARIST (COMMUNION), CONFIRMATION, MARRIAGE, ORDINATION, AND EXTREME UNCTION (ANOINTING OF THE SICK, OR LAST RITES). THREE OF THE SACRAMENTS CAN BE RECEIVED ONLY ONCE IN A LIFETIME BECAUSE THEY MAKE AN INDELIBLE "SACRAMENTAL CHARACTER" OR MARK ON A PERSON'S SOUL: THESE THREE ARE BAPTISM, CONFIRMATION, AND ORDINATION. IN ORDINATION, A MAN MAY LATER BE ORDAINED TO A HIGHER RANK OF THE PRIESTHOOD BUT HE MAY NOT BE ORDAINED TWICE ON THE SAME LEVEL. MARRIAGE MAY BE PERFORMED MORE THAN ONCE BUT ONLY AFTER THE DEATH OF ONE OF THE PARTNERS.

RIGHT Baptism is the entry point into the Catholic Church. A baby is usually baptized within a month of being born. However, converts to Catholicism can be baptized at any age. No other sacraments can be proffered without baptism first.

BELOW Pope Benedict XVI leads a ceremony for the ordination of 21 new Catholic priests in St Peter's Basilica.

Baptism is the process through which a person enters the Catholic Church by washing away all sins, including "original sin" (the sin of Adam and Eve in eating the fruit from the Tree of Knowledge in the Garden of Eden). Generally, baptism is administered to babies but it can be performed at any age. The sacrament of confession – or penance and reconciliation – is the acknowledgement of sins committed. Sins are confessed to a priest who, in the name of Christ, will set a penance that leads to absolution. The penitent must be truly sorry for his or her sin and willing to make restitution where necessary.

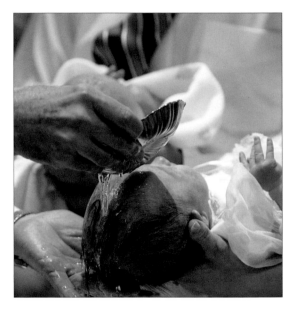

The Holy Eucharist is the receiving of the body and blood of Christ to enter into union with Christ. Confirmation is the sacrament conferring grace and strength to be a perfect Christian. It is mostly administered when a child is old enough to understand it – generally between the ages of seven and 15 – and it can only be offered to those who are baptized. In the Protestant Church, confirmation must precede communion, but in the Catholic Church a child can go to confession and communion from about the age of seven onward, before confirmation takes place. The sacred union of a man and woman in the sight of God is the sacrament of marriage. In Catholicism, marriage

is for life and, if a couple should get a legal divorce, neither could marry again in a church. A marriage can be annulled in exceptional circumstances – with evidence that one or both partners had no intention, at the time of the wedding, for the marriage to be for life. Ordination, or holy orders, is entering the priesthood. This involves a vow of lifetime celibacy and is a sacrament available to only men in the Catholic Church. Lastly, extreme unction is the anointing with oil of a person who is sick or dying, in order to confer Christ's grace and strength. It can be administered before a serious operation or at any time when life may be threatened, and it may be given several times.

THE MASS

The central act of Catholic worship is the Mass. It is a celebration of the Last Supper that Jesus ate with his disciples before being arrested in the Garden of Gethsemane but, more importantly, it is an acknowledgement of Christ's sacrifice for mankind through the crucifixion. Catholic priests and the most observant of their flocks celebrate Mass every day; the Mass is said to carry the cross until Christ returns. Originally known only as the "Holy Eucharist", it became generally known as *missa*, or "Mass", in the late 4th century AD. After many amendments over the centuries, Pope Pius VI attempted to standardize it at a General Council in 1570, so that heretical notions linked to the surge of Protestantism in Europe did not infiltrate the rite. It was named "Tridentine" after

Trent, the Italian town where the council met. The Second Vatican Council in the 1960s simplified the Mass and allowed it to be conducted in each country's national language as well as in Latin.

THE ROSARY

The term Rosary derives from the Latin *rosarium*, meaning "crown of roses". It is a traditional form of Catholic devotion involving a string of prayer beads with a crucifix and a recital of set prayers. Catholics "pray the Rosary" to remember 20 mysteries of salvation. These are divided into the five Joyful Mysteries, the five Luminous Mysteries, the five Sorrowful Mysteries and the five Glorious Mysteries, each of which are represented by beads.

Prayers, including the "Our Father" and the "Hail Mary", are repeated as the supplicant contemplates the mysteries. Pope John Paul II's Apostolic Letter of 16 October 2002, "Rosarium Virginis Mariae", suggests that the Joyful Mysteries should be said on Monday and Saturday, the Luminous on Thursday, the Sorrowful on Tuesday and Friday, and the Glorious on Wednesday and Sunday. Sundays of Christmas season, however, belong to the Joyful Mysteries and Sundays of Lent to the Sorrowful Mysteries. Before John Paul II's Apostolic Letter, 15 decades (multiples of ten) were said instead of his recommended 20.

LEFT Catholics make vows for life when they marry in church. However, a marriage can be annulled if one of the partners can prove that they had no intention of keeping their vows at the time that they were made. The marriage is then deemed never to have happened.

ABOVE The rosary is a constant reminder of a Catholic's faith, with each bead depicting a set routine of prayer that is followed regularly throughout the day. The prayers include the "Lord's Prayer" and the "Hail Mary".

LEFT A priest raises the holy cup containing wine for the Mass, depicting the Last Supper. For many years in Catholic churches the congregation only ate the holy wafers, with priests drinking the wine, but now, as in the Protestant Church, the congregants may both drink the wine and eat the wafer.

MONASTIC LIFE

IN CATHOLICISM, THE "SACRED MARRIAGE" IS THE RELATIONSHIP BETWEEN GOD AND HIS CHURCH. DURING THE EARLY YEARS OF CHRISTIANITY, MANY PEOPLE MADE VOWS OF CHASTITY AND DEVOTED THEIR LIVES TO CHRIST. ST THECLA, A FOLLOWER OF ST PAUL IN THE 1ST CENTURY, WAS ONE OF THE FIRST WOMEN TO DO SO. HOWEVER, THE CHRISTIAN MONASTIC LIFE OFFICIALLY BEGAN WITH ST ANTHONY, WHO GAVE UP A LIFE OF RICHES IN THE 3RD CENTURY TO LIVE AN ASCETIC, CELIBATE LIFE OF WORSHIP IN THE DESERT OUTSIDE ALEXANDRIA. TODAY THERE ARE MANY RELIGIOUS MONASTIC ORDERS, INCLUDING SEVERAL IN THE ANGLICAN CHURCH. TO REFLECT THE IDEA THAT THESE MEN AND WOMEN ARE WEDDED TO THE CHURCH, NUNS ARE OFTEN REFERRED TO AS "BRIDES OF CHRIST".

RIGHT Monte Cassino Monastery in Italy as it is today. It was here that St Benedict of Norcia founded the first Benedictine Monastery in c. AD529. The abbey was badly damaged by warfare over the centuries and finally destroyed in 1944. It was rebuilt after the war and re-consecrated in 1964.

BELOW Benedictine nuns of the Convent of Perpetual Adoration gather in a room and read from their devotional books in Kansas City, Missouri.

The Catholic Church bases its ruling on the celibacy of priests on the biblical implication that Jesus Christ was not married. However, Catholic priests were not required to become celibate until some time after the 4th century AD, when the Council of Elvira in Spain forbade all bishops, priests and deacons to marry. There is evidence that the majority of priests before then did not marry, but there was confusion about the meaning of the word "celibate", which, in the first 500 years AD, meant "unmarried" rather than "not having sexual relations". During that time, many unmarried priests had relationships with women.

At the beginning of the 11th century, Pope Benedict VIII brought in stronger laws to support clerical celibacy and made it impossible for the children of priests to inherit property. However, the first written law that priests should never marry, dates from the Second Lateran Council in 1139, and the Council of Trent in 1570 reaffirmed this.

In exceptional circumstances, and with Papal permission, some men who are already married can be admitted into the Catholic priesthood. For example, Anglican priests who in recent years objected to the ordination of women in the Protestant Church, were permitted to convert and become Catholic priests. Should any one of them become widowed, however, they would not be allowed to marry again and remain a priest.

MONKS AND NUNS

The word "monk" comes from the Greek *monachos*, meaning solitary or lonely person. Nowadays the monastic life is almost always associated with seclusion in a monastery or convent, but religious ascetics have lived hermit-like, celibate lives since ancient times. In the time of Jesus, the celibate Essenes (all male) lived at Qumran by the Dead Sea in an area that is now known as Israel, and the Therapeutae (men and women living separately) lived a monastic life outside Alexandria. Followers of Eastern religions and paganism have long done the same.

Western monastic life began with St Benedict (AD480–547), who founded the first monastery at Monte Cassino, Italy, in AD529, where monks and nuns lived separately. During the Middle Ages, there was corruption in wealthy monasteries and convents due to the sale of Indulgences and prayers, the occurrence of sexual misconduct, and the "buying" of promotions. During the Reformation, Henry VIII saw his opportunity to confiscate the wealth of monasteries and convents, and closed them down, whether they were corrupt or pure. This meant the end of hundreds of centres of hospitality, medical care and learning, and led to the loss of thousands of precious manuscripts and icons. Monastic life became illegal in Britain until the 19th century. In Catholic Europe, monastic life thrived and grew for another century but has become less popular since the 1950s. Today, there are more Buddhist monks and nuns than Christian ones, even though Catholicism is the most commonly held religious faith in the world.

MONASTIC LIFE TODAY

There are more than 1,000 Catholic monastic orders worldwide, the vast majority of which are for women. They consist of 25 different orders, the best known being Franciscan (including Poor Clares), Carmelite, Augustinian, Benedictine, Cistercian (including Trappists) and Dominican.

Each one is slightly different in following the life and recommendations of its founder, but all monks and nuns take vows of poverty, chastity and obedience and must commit to following the commandments of the Church. Monks and nuns live in monasteries or convents and are self-supporting through their own work or through donations. Many of these institutions are "enclosed", meaning that the monks or nuns stay inside the monastery walls, devoting the rest of their lives to contemplation, work and prayer. They do not marry or own possessions. The monastic day revolves around eight "offices", which include prayers, psalms, Bible readings, services and song. These are often known as "Opus Dei" – the work of God. The litany of services is: 2 a.m. Matins, 5 a.m. Lauds, 7 a.m. Prime, 9 a.m. Terce, 12 p.m. Sext, 3 p.m. None, 5 p.m. Vespers, 8 p.m. Compline.

ABOVE St Benedict praying with his monks. Benedict founded his monastery on an earlier shrine to the Greek god Apollo, and his first action was to smash the god's statue and altar and re-dedicate the site to St John the Baptist. Benedict's twin sister, St Scholastica, founded the first convent for women about five miles away from Monte Cassino.

BELOW A young Franciscan monk serves lunch at a monastery in the state of Querétaro, central Mexico.

VENERATION OF SAINTS

THE FIRST DAYS OF CHRISTIANITY WERE FRAUGHT WITH DANGER AND MANY FOLLOWERS OF CHRIST WERE KILLED FOR THEIR FAITH. THESE MARTYRS, IT WAS BELIEVED, WENT DIRECTLY TO HEAVEN AND, THROUGH THEIR OWN HOLINESS, COULD ASSIST IN OBTAINING GRACE AND BLESSINGS FOR OTHERS. IN THE SAME WAY THAT THE JEWS HONOURED PROPHETS AND HOLY PEOPLE, CHRISTIAN MARTYRS WERE VENERATED WITH FESTIVAL DAYS AND SEEN AS EXAMPLES OF FAITH AND HOLY LIVING.

RIGHT The holy blessing of pet animals in New York, on the annual feast of St Francis of Assisi: all types of pets are presented at St John the Divine church.

BELOW Pope John Paul II visiting the sacred shrine of the Virgin Mary at Lourdes, France. The shrine is the place where St Bernadette, a shepherd girl, saw 18 visions of the Holy Mother in 1858. Although it is a shrine of healing visited by millions, St Bernadette herself died from tuberculosis at the age of 35.

St Stephen was the first Christian martyr, and was stoned to death by a crowd in the 1st century AD. The first non-martyred saint was St John the Evangelist, one of Jesus' apostles, who is believed to have been exiled to the Greek island of Patmos. Saints often became patrons of specific attributes such as countries, occupations or sicknesses. One of the best-known patron saints is St Francis of Assisi whose "Canticle of the Creatures" and love of wildlife and nature earned him the title of patron saint of animals. St Jude is the patron saint of hopeless causes because his New Testament letter stresses the importance of perseverance in difficult times. St Matthew, the tax-gatherer who became a disciple of Jesus, is the patron saint of accountants and tax gatherers. Patron saints can be given modern attributes, too. St Clare of Assisi is

patron saint of television because she had a vision of Christmas Mass from her sick bed, although the church where it was taking place was elsewhere.

HOW TO BECOME A SAINT

Formal canonization (or selection) of saints began in the 10th century. Before then, saints were chosen by public demand and many were purely legendary beings. Originally, four miracles had to be established before the first stage of becoming a saint – beatification – with a further two miracles being demonstrated before canonization, but Pope John Paul II simplified this process in 1983. Nowadays the local bishop begins an investigation into the candidate's life for heroic virtue and orthodoxy of doctrine, before passing details on to theologians at the Vatican. After initial approval, the candidate is pronounced "venerable". Beatification requires evidence of one miracle (except in the case of martyrs).

This miracle must take place after the death of the candidate as proof that they are in heaven and have interceded after they have been petitioned in prayer. Once beatification takes place, the candidate is known as "the blessed" and may be venerated by his or her followers. One further miracle is required for canonization. Once sainthood is conferred, it is irrevocable.

MARIAN PRINCIPLE

Mary, mother of Jesus, is venerated throughout the Catholic world. Catholics emphasize that the Virgin Mary is the first of the saints, and since she was human, she is not worshipped. However, the adoration of the Virgin is a profound part of Catholic theology and Mary is constantly asked to intercede for people in their prayers. The distinction is often difficult for non-Catholics to understand.

That Mary was born and died a virgin is accepted dogma in the Catholic Church. Catholics also believe in the Assumption, in which Mary was bodily admitted into heaven when she died, and that she is honoured as Queen there. The "Regina Coeli" (Queen of Heaven) is an anthem used in Catholic churches at Eastertime. Mary was declared to be the "Mother of God" by the Christian church in the 5th century at Ephesus, Turkey. Detractors of the Church have pointed out that Ephesus was a centre of worship of the pagan mother-goddess, Artemis, one of whose titles was also "Queen of Heaven". Another pagan Queen of Heaven features in the Old Testament's book of Jeremiah.

Visions of the Virgin Mary have appeared to thousands of people – especially to children – around the world. Her best-known sacred shrines are at Lourdes in France, Fatima in Portugal and Guadalupe in Mexico. Pope John Paul II was devoted to the Virgin Mary: his motto, *Totus Tuus* (totally yours), was dedicated to her and his personal coat of arms contained the letter "M", representing Mary at the foot of the Cross.

LEFT An Ave Maria prayer card. *Ave Maria* is Latin for "Hail Mary" and appears in many forms throughout the Church, especially in music. The first line of the prayer is the salutation of the Virgin by the Archangel Gabriel, from the Gospel of Luke, and the second line is the greeting given to Mary by Elizabeth, mother of John the Baptist. Mary is often referred to as "Our Lady of the Rosary".

HAIL MARY PRAYER

The Hail Mary is the best known and possibly the best loved of the prayers of the Catholic Church.
Hail Mary, full of grace,
The Lord is with thee.
Blessed art thou among women,
And blessed is the fruit of thy womb, Jesus.
Holy Mary, Mother of God,
Pray for us sinners now and at the hour of
our death.
Amen.

IMMACULATE CONCEPTION

The Immaculate Conception is a Catholic dogma that asserts that the soul of the Virgin Mary was conceived without the stigma of original sin and that she lived an earthly life completely free from sin. It is frequently confused with the concept of the Virgin Birth but refers only to the state of Mary's soul; her conception and birth were biologically normal. The Feast of the Immaculate Conception was originally an Eastern Catholic festival, first celebrated in the West in the 8th century but officially recognized in 1483. However, it was not enforced as a doctrine of faith until 1854.

BELOW *The Immaculate Conception* by Giovanni Battista Tiepolo, in the Museo del Prado, Madrid, Spain. It is now a dogma of the Catholic Church that the Virgin Mary was born without original sin so that she would be pure enough to bear the Christ.

THE POPE

THE POPE IS A NON-HEREDITARY, ELECTED MONARCH WITH ABSOLUTE AUTHORITY OVER THE CATHOLIC CHURCH. HIS OFFICIAL TITLE IS THE BISHOP OF ROME, BUT OVER THE CENTURIES THE WORD "POPE", FROM THE LATIN *PAPA* AND GREEK *PAPPAS*, MEANING "FATHER", HAS COME TO BE THE ACCEPTED TITLE. THE OFFICE OF THE POPE IS CALLED THE "PAPACY"; HIS ECCLESIASTICAL JURISDICTION IS CALLED THE HOLY SEE. THE HOME OF THE HOLY SEE IS THE VATICAN, WHICH IS A SOVEREIGN STATE IN ITS OWN RIGHT AND THE SMALLEST INDEPENDENT NATION STATE IN THE WORLD.

ABOVE Pope Benedict XVI waves to the faithful at the end of his first general audience in St Peter's Square at the Vatican.

RIGHT St Peter's Basilica in Vatican City, Rome. Although not the official ecclesiastical seat of the pope (St John Lateran is), it is most certainly his principal church. Most papal ceremonies take place at St Peter's due to its size, proximity to the papal residence and location within Vatican City's walls.

ELECTION OF THE POPE

A new pope is elected by a College of Cardinals who meet, behind closed doors, in the Sistine Chapel in Rome. This ancient ritual is known as a conclave and takes place between 15 and 20 days after the death of the pope. In theory, the cardinals can elect any baptized male Catholic to the position but, in reality, the new pope is always a cardinal. Open campaigning is forbidden, but the selection of a new pope is still a very political process. The vote is made in written ballots and the papers are burnt, giving off a dark grey smoke from the chimney of the Sistine Chapel. A final decision is made when two-thirds of all the cardinals agree. Then, a chemical is added to the papers, which creates white smoke instead of grey, and the bells of St Peter's Basilica ring out to announce the election of a new pope.

Vatican City, the home of the Vatican, is situated on land considered sacred since before the time of Christ. Originally known as Ager Vatinarus and Mons Vaticanus (Vatican Fields and Vatican Hill) it was divided from the city of Rome by the Tiber river. St Peter is believed to have been buried there, and the first church was built over his tomb in the 4th century. The current St Peter's Basilica, built between 1506 and 1626, is one of the largest churches in Christianity, covering more than five acres and capable of holding more than 60,000 people. The Apostolic Palace, located next to St Peter's Basilica, is the official residence of the pope, and it also contains the Vatican Museum, the Vatican Library and the Sistine Chapel with its famous ceiling frescoes painted by Michelangelo.

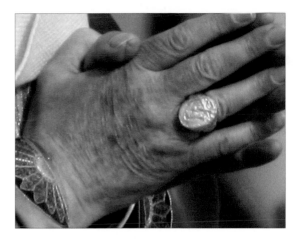

BELOW Pope Benedict XVI clasps his hands, showing his papal ring, during his inaugural Mass in St Peter's Square on 24 April 2005.

BENEDICT XVI AND JOHN PAUL II

Pope Benedict XVI, born Joseph Ratzinger in Bavaria, was elected as the 265th pope in April 2005. Joseph Ratzinger began training for the priesthood immediately after the end of the Second World War and was ordained in 1951. In 1981, Pope John Paul II made him prefect of the Congregation for the Doctrine of the Faith, formerly known as the Holy Office of the Historical Inquisition, where he taught on topics such as birth control, homosexuality and inter-religious dialogue. He became known for his disciplinary measures against some liberal theologians in Latin America in the 1980s.

His predecessor, the Polish-born Karol Wojtyla, was elected Pope John Paul II in 1978, after the sudden death of John Paul I who reigned for just over one month. John Paul II was the third longest-serving pope in history and the most widely travelled, visiting more than 120 countries during his 26-year papacy. In 1981, a Turkish man, Mehmet Ali Agca, shot the pope twice in an assassination attempt. John Paul II forgave him and visited him in prison. John Paul II's death in 2005 was publicly mourned by millions, and his funeral was the first one of a pope to be shown on live television around the world.

PAPAL INFALLIBILITY

The doctrine of Papal Infallibility dates back to before the Middle Ages but was not completely defined until the First Vatican Council of 1870. It is limited to definitive and binding pronouncements by the pope on faith and morals. These are rarely given, but to conservative Catholics such statements are as infallible as the Bible. The most recent use of Papal Infallibility was the announcement of the dogma of the Assumption of Mary by Pope Pius XII in 1950. Papal Infallibility does not mean that the Pope is necessarily divinely inspired nor exempt from the possibility of sin.

VATICAN II

The Second Vatican Council, or Vatican II, was a theological and ecumenical congress lasting for four consecutive autumns during 1962–5. Its aim was to promote spiritual renewal while considering the Church's position in the modern world. The Council decided to allow Mass in the language of the congregation rather than in Latin. It also acknowledged the validity of other religions and granted the laity an enhanced role in church, including reading scripture and giving communion.

ABOVE The Second Vatican Council, an ecclesiastical congress of more than 2,500 bishops from around the world that lasted for four consecutive autumns during 1962–5. It was convened by Pope John XXIII but concluded by his successor, Pope Paul VI.

BELOW This fresco from the chapel of the Château de la Verrerie in Aubigny, France, depicts Jesus giving Peter the keys to the Kingdom of Heaven. Catholic doctrine states that Jesus appointed St Peter to be the first pope.

ST PETER, THE FIRST POPE

Simon, a fisherman born in the Galilean village of Bethsaida, was one of the first disciples. Jesus renamed him Peter (from the Greek word *petros*, meaning "rock") and stated "on this rock I shall build my church" (Matthew 16:18). Following the Resurrection, Peter travelled far, teaching the words of Jesus. According to legend, Peter was martyred in Rome, insisting on being crucified upside down, as he deemed himself unworthy to meet the same death as his Lord.

CONTROVERSIES

THE MOST INFAMOUS POPE IN HISTORY WAS POPE ALEXANDER VI (1492–1503), THE FORMER RODRIGO BORGIA, WHO HAD SEVEN OPENLY ACKNOWLEDGED ILLEGITIMATE CHILDREN WHILE HE WAS A CARDINAL. AS THE NEWLY ELECTED POPE, HE ALSO HAD AN AFFAIR WITH A 19-YEAR-OLD MARRIED WOMAN. THE FIRST MEDICI POPE, GIOVANNI DE' MEDICI – LEO X – BECAME LEGENDARY FOR OFFERING MEALS OF 65 COURSES OR MORE. HUNDREDS OF POEMS WERE WRITTEN IN HONOUR OF LEO'S FAVOURITE PET, A WHITE ELEPHANT, AND THE VATICAN LIBRARY CONTAINS A DIARY OF THE ELEPHANT'S SOCIAL ENGAGEMENTS.

BELOW The Female Pontiff, or Pope Joan, from a 17th-century pack of Tarot cards, Venice. Pope Joan is probably an invention, possibly originating as an anti-papal satire.

RIGHT Pope Leo X (the first Medici pope) was legendary for offering meals of 65 courses or more. He had a pet white elephant called Hanno, which was the origin of the phrase "a white elephant", meaning something that is useless but costly to maintain.

The most controversial pope was undoubtedly Pope Joan – but her existence is legend. She is said to have reigned from 853 to 855, and her story first became known through the writings of a 13th-century man, Martin of Opava. Joan was alleged to have dressed as a man and to have studied with unequalled dedication . Joan (or John Anglicius, as she was allegedly known in public) was elected pope but reigned for less than three years. She became pregnant and, through ignorance of the exact time when the baby was expected, gave birth while in a papal procession in Rome. Some writers ascribe the legendary Pope Joan to the 10th century and say that she was stoned to death after the birth of the baby; others say that she was deposed and finished her life in a convent.

THE SOCIETY OF JESUS

The Jesuits were founded in Spain in 1534 by St Ignatius Loyola. He was a soldier who had lived a life of excess but, after being wounded, dedicated himself to becoming a soldier of the Catholic faith and wrote the famous book *Spiritual Exercises*. The Jesuits were zealous missionaries who made as many enemies as friends, with a legendary reputation that linked them with inquisitorial tendencies. The tide turned against the Jesuits in the 18th century as Protestantism spread, and they were banished from several countries. In 1773, Pope Clement

XIV abolished them entirely, but they were reinstated by Pius VII in 1814. They were not popular with Pope John Paul II, however, and the alleged preference of both him and the current Pope, Benedict XVI, for Opus Dei has exacerbated rumours of ill-feeling between the two groups.

SCANDAL

The most serious scandal linked to the Catholic Church in the late 20th and early 21st centuries concerns sexual abuse. A survey commissioned by the US bishops' National Review Board showed that more than 4,000 clergymen in the USA were accused of sexual abuse with a minor between 1950 and 2002.

Other cases of abuse have also been confirmed in Europe. The Catholic Church has stated that it considers the sexual abuse of children to be a mortal sin. A person dying with unremitted mortal sin on their conscience is viewed as being in danger of eternal separation from God in hell.

FINANCES

The Vatican's revenues come from four sources: dioceses and other ecclesiastical entities, property, publishing and investment income. The Vatican Bank is the common name for the Institute for Religious Works, which is the central bank for the Catholic Church, based in Vatican City. The Vatican Bank was involved in a major financial and political scandal in the 1980s, as it was a shareholder in another bank, Banco Ambrosiano, which was accused of money laundering. Banco Ambrosiano collapsed owing up to a billon dollars, and its chairman, Roberto Calvi, was murdered in 1982.

The wealth of the Vatican has been subject to centuries of speculation, and there have been allegations of links with the mafia,

Nazi investments in Eastern Europe and right-wing governments, and rumours that the Vatican Bank gave money to the Polish group Solidarity. There have also been accusations of investment in businesses contrary to Church teachings, such as contraceptive manufacturing companies and armaments trading. None of the allegations have been substantiated. It is known that Mussolini paid the Church $80 million for property confiscated from it in the 19th century and that that money has been invested since. The portfolio is thought to be worth approximately $1.5 billion.

SECRETS

The Vatican Library was founded in the 4th century but was little used until the 15th century. It holds more than 75,000 manuscripts and more than one million printed books. The Vatican Archives contain a separate collection of more than 150,000 items, including coins and medals.

The precious and ancient documents that are known to be in the library include an illuminated copy of part of the Koran, from Tunis, dating back to 1535, and the four Gospels in Coptic and Arabic, dating back to the monastery of St Anthony and copied in 1205. In the 1990s, Michael Baigent and Richard Leigh's book *The Dead Sea Scrolls Deception* alleged that some of the scrolls had been hidden in the Vatican Library to suppress allegations that St Paul faked the story of Jesus. According to other theories, the library holds details of known Catholic paedophiles and other wrong-doings associated with the Church.

LEFT The interior of the Vatican Library. It has been suggested that the Catholic Church keeps documents in the library that disprove most or all of its doctrines and beliefs. Some parts of the library require special permission to enter, hence the reputation for secrecy.

BELOW St Ignatius Loyola, founder of the Jesuits. Ignatius was a soldier and a lover of the good things in life until an injury in battle forced him to re-think his life. The Jesuits originated the phrase "give me a boy until he is seven and I will give you the man".

BIRTH CONTROL

The Catholic Church is morally opposed to all forms of contraception apart from "natural family planning" – the refraining from sexual intercourse during times when conception is likely to take place. This ruling was enforced by Pope Paul's ruling "Humanae Vitae" in 1968, when he opposed the new contraceptive pill. Since then, more controversy has arisen over the spread of AIDS, particularly in African countries, and the scientific view that condoms help prevent AIDS-related deaths.

PART TWO

THE FOUNDER

 Josemaría Escrivá de Balaguer, a controversial and charismatic Spanish priest, was just 26 years old when he claimed to have received direct inspiration from God to found Opus Dei, which means "the work of God" in Latin. The Work, as it is called by members of Opus Dei, is to sanctify daily work, no matter how mundane, to spread the word of Christ and to endeavour to live the life of a saint. Escrivá devoted the rest of his life to the creation and expansion of Opus Dei and, 27 years after his death in 1975, he was canonized as a saint by Pope John Paul II.

RIGHT Josemaría Escrivá carried out two catechetical journeys to South America in 1974 and 1975. The latter was cut short by illness, which forced him to return to Rome. Here, he is addressing a gathering of thousands of people in Buenos Aires.

THE EARLY YEARS

THE FOUNDER

JOSEMARÍA ESCRIVÁ WAS BORN IN 1902, THE FIRST SON OF A PROSPEROUS, MIDDLE-CLASS AND DEEPLY PIOUS SPANISH FAMILY, WHO LIVED IN BARBASTRO IN ARAGON, SPAIN. HE HAD ONE MUCH YOUNGER BROTHER AND FOUR SISTERS, THREE OF WHOM DIED DURING CHILDHOOD. WHEN JOSEMARÍA WAS TWO YEARS OLD, HE BECAME CRITICALLY ILL. HE RECOVERED ONLY AFTER HIS MOTHER, DOLORES, VOWED TO TAKE HIM TO THE 11TH-CENTURY SHRINE OF THE VIRGIN MARY IN TORRECIUDAD.

ABOVE Josemaría's parents, José Escrivá (1867–1924) and Dolores Albás (1877–1941). They had three children who survived to adulthood: Carmen, Josemaría and Santiago.

RIGHT Josemaría, aged two. When he was taken seriously ill with a fever, his mother promised the Virgin Mary that if he got better, she would take him to the shrine of Our Lady of Torreciudad. She kept her promise and made the perilous journey to the shrine on horseback.

The Escrivá family's business in Barbastro failed when Josemaría was 13, and they had to give up having servants (unheard-of for a middle-class Spanish family of the time), and move to a much smaller home in the town of Logroño. Here, Josemaría's father, Don José, went into partnership in a clothes shop called La Gran Ciudad de Londres (the Great City of London). Escrivá's first school, in Barbastro, was run by a priestly order known as the Piarist Fathers. When his family moved to Logroño, he attended a state school in the mornings and St Anthony's tutorial college in the afternoons. Despite his religious upbringing, Escrivá's first ambition was to be an architect.

In his early life, Escrivá had a variety of names. His baptismal record lists him as José María Escribá y Albás (the "b" instead of a "v" was a mistake by the priest). He chose to merge his two Christian names as a symbol of the marriage between Joseph and Mary and added "de Balaguer", so that his full name became Josemaría Escrivá de Balaguer y Albás. The "y Albás", which was his mother's maiden name, later fell out of usage as did "de Balaguer". Opus Dei now refer to him as St Josemaría Escrivá.

VOCATION

Escrivá's first mystical experience occurred between Christmas and Epiphany 1917–18 when he was deeply moved by the sight of footprints left behind in the snow by a barefoot Carmelite friar. Already religious, he began attending Mass every day.

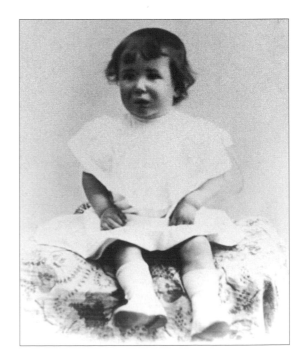

OBTAINING A FAMILY TITLE

To enable Escrivá to train for the priesthood, his family put themselves through years of deprivation. As a way of making up to his family for this sacrifice, Escrivá petitioned for, and was granted, the title of Marqués de Paralta in 1968 so that he could pass it on to his brother, Santiago. Although he explained that doing so was distasteful to him, Escrivá's critics saw this as a self-aggrandizing action, even though he never used the title, and had it transferred to his brother by a judicial act in 1972.

LEFT Josemaría aged 19, a student at the Zaragoza seminary. He was ordained as a priest in the seminary's chapel on 28 March 1925 and three days later sent to the rural village of Perdiguera to substitute for a priest who was ill. Josemaría's first duty as a priest was to clean the church from end to end.

Escrivá decided that his calling was to become a priest, but he worried that this would bring hardship on his family. However, when his brother Santiago Escrivá was born the following year he realized that there would now be two boys to take care of the family, and he could follow his vocation with a clear conscience.

Escrivá began training for the priesthood at the Catholic seminary in Logroño in 1918. After a year he moved to Zaragoza seminary as a student, living on the campus. He studied for a canon and civil law degree at the city's university at the same time so that he would be able to teach law, to finance himself, while he continued to train for the priesthood. Most often, trainee priests are supported financially through allegiance to and sponsorship from a bishop and diocese, but Escrivá was unusual in that he chose to be independent and earn his own living while also a student.

In 1924, when his young brother was still only five years old, and only a few months before his own ordination, Escrivá's father died, leaving him as the family's main breadwinner. He moved to Madrid in 1927 to pursue a doctorate in law, simultaneously teaching Roman and canon law at a nearby academy. While he was there, he also became chaplain to the Apostolic Ladies of the Sacred Heart of Jesus, a newly created order of nuns who worked among the sick and poor of Madrid. It was during his time both living and working there that he received the inspiration for founding Opus Dei.

FAR LEFT With his sister Carmen and younger brother Santiago (born 28 February 1919). Josemaría's other three sisters, Lolita, Rosario and Asunción (who was nicknamed Chon), all died in infancy. Josemaría was himself a sickly child and, later in life, became a diabetic.

BELOW Josemaría, with students and staff of Zaragoza University Law Faculty (third row, last on right).

THE VISION

ON 2 OCTOBER 1928, ESCRIVÁ ATTENDED A SILENT RETREAT WITH THE ORDER OF VINCENTIAN FATHERS IN MADRID. HE WAS ORGANIZING SOME NOTES AND RESOLUTIONS THAT HE HAD WRITTEN DOWN AS AN AID TO MEDITATION WHEN HE SUDDENLY SAW A VISION OF OPUS DEI: WHAT GOD WANTED IT TO BE AND HOW IT WAS TO BE CARRIED OUT. AT THAT MOMENT, AS IF TO CONFIRM HIS INSPIRATION, A PEAL OF BELLS RANG OUT FROM A NEARBY CHURCH TO LAUNCH THE FEAST OF THE GUARDIAN ANGELS.

RIGHT Josemaría Escrivá with Álvaro del Portillo, the first prelate of Opus Dei, a few months after the end of the Civil War (1939).

BELOW Josemaría (centre) with a group of students on the terrace of the DYA Academy 1935–6.

A plaque has since been placed in the façade of the belfry of the (rebuilt) Church of Our Lady of the Angels, which reads, in Latin: "As the bells of the Madrid Church of Our Lady of the Angels rang out and raised their voices in praise to the heavens, on 2 October 1928, Josemaría Escrivá de Balaguer received in his mind and heart the seeds of Opus Dei."

From that time onward, Escrivá devoted himself body and soul to the development of The Work, even though he stated that he did not want to be the founder of anything. His vision had inspired him to believe that the Catholic Church was in need of revitalization, with the focus on the

sanctification of work, whether it was rocket science or road sweeping. Opus Dei was to be a focal point for Catholics who wanted to re-commit to their faith, making their lives holy in every moment and honouring every Catholic dogma with total obedience.

Escrivá's vision included both priests and lay people. He did not believe that priests were superior to those who carried out everyday work or raised families, and he wanted people from all walks of life to feel they belonged to a committed Catholic family that shared principles and community.

Escrivá began to write to friends and colleagues outlining the idea of Opus Dei. His unquenchable belief in The Work was infectious, and his strength of vision and character soon attracted others to the cause. Over the next five years, he gathered around him priests and laymen with a passionate love of Jesus Christ who would meet together in a café called El Sotanillo ("little basement") in Madrid. Escrivá talked to them about Opus Dei and took them on visits to the poor and sick, setting up classes in the catechism (belief system) of the Catholic Church in poorer areas.

THE FIRST MEMBERS

In 1930, Isidoro Zorzano, an engineer and former school friend of Escrivá's in Logroño, became the first person to ask to be admitted formally to Opus Dei as a lay member; others followed. The founder wanted to create a civil entity of unified thought with a Christian spirit. Escrivá set up the DYA Academy in 1933, teaching the principles of Opus Dei simultaneously with classes in law and architecture. DYA officially stood for Derecho y Arquitectura (Law and Architecture), but for Escrivá and his students, it stood for *Dios y audacia* ("God and daring"). It was a place for spiritual direction for students, and

this grew to include housing for the students who were interested in the principles of Opus Dei, whether or not they wished to join the group officially. He also began to draw up documents defining the spirit and way of doing things for generations to come.

Three of the original members, Álvaro del Portillo, José María Hernández de Garnica, and José Luis Múzquiz, were ordained as priests in 1944. Escrivá did not attend their ordination. He explained his reasons some years later: "My role is to hide and disappear, so that only Jesus shines forth." Álvaro del Portillo was Escrivá's closest collaborator and succeeded him as leader of Opus Dei on his death in June 1975.

ABOVE Josemaría with the first three members of Opus Dei to be ordained to the priesthood, shortly before their ordination. All three were engineers. Left to right: José Luis Múzquiz, José María Hernández de Garnica, Josemaría Escrivá and Álvaro del Portillo.

BELOW The first three members of Opus Dei after ordination, conferred by Dr Eijo y Garay, Bishop of Madrid.

THE SPANISH CIVIL WAR

IN 1936, THE SPANISH CIVIL WAR BROKE OUT. GENERAL FRANCISCO FRANCO LED A RIGHT-WING, PRO-CATHOLIC, NATIONALIST REBELLION AGAINST THE LEFT-WING SECOND SPANISH REPUBLIC. THE REPUBLICANS RETALIATED WITH MASSACRES OF CATHOLIC CLERGY AND THE BURNING OF CHURCHES, MONASTERIES AND CONVENTS. THE WAR WAS VIEWED AS A BATTLE BETWEEN FASCISM (FRANCO) AND LIBERTY (THE REPUBLICANS), BUT FRANCO'S FOLLOWERS CONSIDERED IT TO BE A BATTLE BETWEEN CHRISTIAN CIVILIZATION AND COMMUNISM.

RIGHT An anti-clerical poster for the socialist trade union UGT (General Workers' Union), which translates "How the Church has sown religion in Spain."

BELOW A burning convent on the Plaza de España in Madrid, April 1931. The Spanish Civil War (1936–9) started with military uprisings throughout Spain and its colonies, followed by Republican reprisals against the Church, viewed as an oppressive institution supportive of the old order. There were massacres of Catholic clergy, and churches, monasteries and convents were burned.

For the Catholics in Spain, it was a terrible time where no one who professed a Christian faith was safe. When Madrid was taken by Republican forces, Escrivá and all the other priests in the city were forced into hiding. Early on in the fighting, the Republicans caught a man they mistakenly thought was Escrivá and hanged him in front of Escrivá's mother's house.

Escrivá was actually hiding in a local mental asylum, run by a friend, feigning mental illness. He later found refuge in the Honduran Consulate, but as time went on, many of the remaining priests decided that they had no alternative but to make the dangerous journey over the Pyrenees into the neutral territory of Andorra and back into the part of Spain run by the Nationalists.

COMO HA SEMBRADO LA IGLESIA SU RELIGION EN ESPAÑA

ESCAPE TO ANDORRA

To make his escape, Escrivá had to leave his mother and sister behind in Madrid and travel first to Barcelona, where groups of refugees gathered to be guided over the mountains by rebels and smugglers who had knowledge of the Pyrenees. It was more than a month before he could find a convoy to take him across to Andorra, by which time he was out of money, exhausted and hungry. The journey involved walking through the snowy mountain passes during the night and hiding in the daytime, with the constant fear of being discovered and shot.

were quick to find ways around the ruling, and both Italy and Germany despatched aeroplanes and troops to support Franco. For Germany, the Spanish Civil War was an ideal opportunity for rearmament behind the scenes — in violation of the First World War peace treaty — as well as an excellent training ground for the Luftwaffe. In this way, Franco, fascism and the Nazis were firmly linked.

LEFT Father Josemaría Escrivá among the ruins of the DYA Academy, 28 March 1939. Opus Dei had only just begun its work before the Spanish Civil War, but it was only buildings that were crushed, not the enthusiasm for The Work.

LOSS OF LIFE

Republican forces killed nearly 7,000 priests and religious people during the Spanish Civil War. Escrivá's home town of Barbastro in Aragon saw 123 of its 140 priests killed; the number in Barcelona was 279; in Valencia, 327; and in Madrid, 1,118. Twelve bishops, 283 nuns and 2,365 monks were also killed. Lay people did not escape either. Some were killed because they were church-goers or wore a religious symbol such as a crucifix. Others lost their lives for granting refuge to clerics. Thousands of churches were burned, religious objects were destroyed and religious tombs were defiled.

ABOVE In Andorra with the group of men who crossed the border over the Pyrenees, 3 December 1937. Josemaría stayed there for a week before crossing into the nationalist zone of Spain, having first gone to Lourdes to thank Our Lady for his safe arrival.

Escrivá's faith gave him strength, and every time the convoy stopped to rest or to hide for a few days, he would introduce himself as a priest and celebrate Mass whenever possible, bringing comfort and hope to his travelling companions. Once over the border, Escrivá travelled to Lourdes to thank the Virgin Mary for his safe passage. Finally, he crossed back into Spain at Hendaye, where he would be safe.

In 1936, Europe set up a non-intervention agreement regarding the Civil War in Spain. However, both Benito Mussolini and Adolf Hitler

LEFT A sketch made by Pedro Casciaro of Father Josemaría during the flight across the Pyrenees. Although the priest had to disguise himself as an ordinary working man for safety, he still offered Mass to all those who wanted it at each stopping place.

POLITICS AND FASCISM

ESCRIVÁ REMAINED RESOLUTELY SILENT ON THE POLITICS OF THE SPANISH CIVIL WAR AND DID NOT COMMENT ON THE OPUS DEI MEMBERS WHO BECAME MEMBERS OF FRANCO'S GOVERNMENT. ESCRIVÁ'S FOLLOWERS AND SOME HISTORIANS HAVE EMPHASIZED HIS EFFORTS TO REMAIN IMPARTIAL IN POLITICS. HE OFTEN STATED THAT OPUS DEI MEMBERS WERE FREE TO FOLLOW WHATEVER POLITICS THEY WISHED.

RIGHT A recruiting poster for anti-fascist forces during the Spanish Civil War.

BELOW Children raise their arms in a fascist salute to a poster of General Franco, which reads "Leader of God and the Mother Country."

Flavio Capucci, postulator of the Cause of Canonization of Josemaría Escrivá, has supported this view and gone on record to say that Opus Dei allows its members the freedom to make their own political decisions. He also pointed out that none of the religious authorities of the time criticized Franco's regime.

Escrivá's followers say that he preached in favour of patriotism, which he defined as love for one's country, as opposed to nationalism, which he said was a disordered love for one's country that led to hatred of other people. The only physical evidence of Escrivá's views comes in a letter that he wrote to General Franco in which he said: "Although a stranger to any political activity, I cannot help but rejoice as a priest and Spaniard that Spain, through its Head of State, has officially accepted the law of God in accordance with the Catholic faith." Despite his stated views on politics, there have been many, mostly unsubstantiated, accusations of

Escrivá's alleged involvement with fascism. These have come partly from Opus Dei's opponents who have often associated the severity of the regulations within the group with fascist tendencies. It has been said that Escrivá believed that all members of Opus Dei should be under the control of leaders and their obedience should be total and unquestioning.

ESCRIVÁ AND THE NAZIS

When questioned about the fascists shortly after the Spanish Civil War, Escrivá is alleged to have said that compared with the communists, at that time, he regarded Hitler's involvement in Spain as the lesser of two evils.

This view is stated in "Trust the Truth", a Catholic Internet blog by a friendly ex-member of Opus Dei, Matthew G. Collins. Vladimir Felzmann, another ex-Opus Dei member, claims that Escrivá insisted that with Hitler's help the Franco Government saved Christianity from communism. He alleges that Escrivá took the view: "Hitler against the Jews, Hitler against the Slavs, this means Hitler against communism."

However, there are several substantiated instances of Escrivá supporting and admiring the Jewish people and, ironically, one of the recurring conspiracy theories about Opus Dei in Spain was that it was a Jewish cult.

OPUS DEI AND FRANCO'S CABINET

Much publicity has been given to the fact that several members of Opus Dei served in Franco's government in the 1960s. In fact, eight of the 113 members of Franco's 11 cabinets, formed between 1939 and 1975, were members of Opus Dei. However, Rafael Calvo Serer, a numerary member of Opus Dei and editor of a daily Madrid newspaper, was forced into exile for his criticisms of Franco's regime, and another numerary, Manuel Fernández Areal, was jailed for publishing critical articles about Franco.

LEFT Francisco Franco y Bahamonde, more commonly known as Generalissimo Francisco Franco, was head of state for a united Spain from 1939 until his death in 1975. During his time in power, he was known officially as *por la gracia de Dios, Caudillo de España y de la Cruzada*, or "by the grace of God, the Leader of Spain and of the Crusade".

A letter from Domingo Diaz-Ambrona, a civil engineer and lawyer to Álvaro del Portillo, prelate of Opus Dei, dated 9 January 1992, published in *Immersed in God,* says that he asked Escrivá for his opinion of the Nazis in the late 1930s. "Here was a priest who had accurate information about the position of the Church and of Catholics in Germany under Hitler's dictatorship. Escrivá spoke very forcefully to me against that anti-Christian regime, and with an energy that clearly showed his great love of freedom. It is necessary to explain that it was not easy, in Spain at that time, to find people who would condemn the Nazi system so categorically or who would denounce its anti-Christian roots with such clarity."

ABOVE Adolf Hitler shakes hands with General Franco at a meeting on the French-Spanish frontier in 1940. Some historians have suggested that Franco made demands that he knew Hitler would not accede to in order to stay out of the Second World War for as long as possible. Spain's fascist government and its support for the Axis powers, particularly Nazi Germany, led to a period of post-war isolation. Spain was not admitted to the United Nations until 1955.

EXPANSION OF OPUS DEI

ESCRIVÁ WAS THE FIRST PRIEST TO RETURN TO MADRID AFTER THE CIVIL WAR ENDED. THE RESIDENCE FOR DYA HAD BEEN COMPLETELY DESTROYED, SO ESCRIVÁ TOOK A ROOM IN AN INN. FROM THERE HE TRACKED DOWN OTHER MEMBERS OF OPUS DEI, VISITED BISHOPS AND PEOPLE OF INFLUENCE, GATHERED BOOKS AND HOLY OBJECTS AND BEGAN THE WORK AGAIN.

ABOVE Josemaría's sister Carmen, who, along with his mother, was of incalculable help to him in the early years. She supervised the domestic tasks of the first centres.

BELOW Escrivá during his first days in Rome.

This time Escrivá was more successful, helped by the promotion of Franco's ultra-conservative "national Catholicism", which taught that being a Catholic was synonymous with being a Spaniard. Also one of the first members of Opus Dei, José María Albareda Herrera, was a personal friend of Franco's Minister of Education.

By the end of 1940, Escrivá had purchased a small hotel, which became a residence for about 20 students, and other centres opened in Valencia, Valladolid and Barcelona.

There was opposition from the Jesuits in both Madrid and Barcelona, with Opus Dei being accused both of being a Jewish sect and having links to the Freemasons, but the claims were ruled to be unfounded by a special tribunal in Madrid.

In 1942, when it still only had about 50 members, Opus Dei was approved as "A Pious Union" – the simplest form of Catholic institution, which simply required the approval of the local bishop. Numbers swelled into the hundreds and, after the Second World War, into the thousands. By the early 1950s, Opus Dei had established centres in Portugal, France, England, Chile, the USA, Mexico, Colombia, Venezuela and Ireland, as well as in Spain.

THE FIRST WOMEN

For the first two years, Escrivá believed that Opus Dei was for men only, but on St Valentine's Day 1930, after celebrating Mass, he became convinced that there should be a women's section. However, it was another six years before a women's branch came into being. In 1948, he established the Roman College of the Holy Cross for men, and on 12 December 1953, Escrivá established the Roman College of Holy Mary for the celibate women of Opus Dei.

MOVING TO ROME

In 1947, Opus Dei was approved as a Secular Institute – a group consisting of both priests and lay people – with the decision confirmed by the Vatican three years later. This gave Escrivá the opportunity to include married people in Opus Dei for the first time. It also meant that the headquarters of the group now had to be in Rome. Escrivá had already moved to Rome

LEFT Escrivá was a man of his time, and when he was a child women rarely worked outside the home after marriage. However, he did not see domestic life as being less vital than other work – rather as a sacred calling. As women became more active in the business world from the 1960s onward, they were also encouraged to develop their business skills in Opus Dei.

himself in 1946. He had been appointed as a "domestic prelate" to the Pope, which gave him the title of Monsignor. He had also obtained a doctorate in theology from the Lateran University and was named consultant to two Vatican Congregations. In a move that surprised many people, he decided that non-Catholics should be allowed to be involved in Opus Dei in the role of "co-operators". As Opus Dei grew throughout the world, he travelled extensively, preaching and teaching and inspiring thousands.

PUBLISHED LITERATURE

Escrivá's first written work was a pamphlet entitled *Consideraciones Espirituales* (Spiritual Thoughts) published in Cuenca, Spain, in 1934 and revised into *Camino* (The Way), his best-known work, five years later. *The Way* is a series of maxims to inspire the seeker of Christ to aspire to holiness in worldly life, and it explains the tenets on which Opus Dei is founded. It is a fierce and controversial book, sometimes contradictory, certainly provocative and can make uncomfortable reading. Example quotes include: "A priest – whoever he may be – is always another Christ", "Let us bless pain, love pain, glorify pain, sanctify pain" and, "Give thanks, as for a very special favour, for that holy abhorrence you feel for yourself". Two years before his death

in 1973, *Christ Is Passing By*, a collection of homilies inspired by holy feast days, was published. *Friends of God*, *Furrow*, *The Forge*, *Conversations*, *In Love with the Church* and *The Way of the Cross* were published posthumously.

ABOVE Josemaría wrote prolifically in his lifetime, though he published relatively little. He sometimes joked about his name: "My name is *Escrivá* and *escribo* [I write]."

CHARISMA AND CHARM

JOSEMARÍA ESCRIVÁ BELIEVED PASSIONATELY IN THE CATHOLIC CHURCH AND ITS MISSION TO SPREAD THE WORD OF GOD. THIS PASSION WAS WHAT DREW PEOPLE TO HIM AND, ALTHOUGH SOME OF HIS VIEWS APPEAR FIERCELY CONSERVATIVE TO THE MORE LIBERAL WORLD OF THE 21ST CENTURY, ESCRIVÁ WAS ESSENTIALLY A MAN OF HIS TIME. HE WAS NOT POLITICALLY CORRECT BY ANY STANDARD, AND IT WAS HIS LACK OF ANY SELF-DOUBT WHATSOEVER THAT EITHER ATTRACTED OR REPELLED HIS LISTENERS.

RIGHT Escrivá was a man driven by his calling. Although he was known for a sense of humour and gentle wit, he was never afraid to speak his mind. As his diabetes caused mood swings, he could be charming one moment and sharp the next.

BELOW Escrivá was at his most charismatic when talking to crowds, and he never lost his enthusiasm for teaching the word of God. No matter how tired his hard-work ethic or illness might make him feel, he was always rejuvenated when it was time to lead a service or to talk about The Work.

Escrivá was a man confident in his conviction of how a spiritual life should be lived. He was sometimes accused of a lack of original thought, but he had the ability to charm and attract, which stemmed from his passion for The Work and his complete devotion to Christ and to the Virgin Mary. Even some of his detractors acknowledge his charm and personality.

However, the people of Aragon are legendary for their fierce tempers and stubbornness and Escrivá was no exception to the rule. He knew what he believed and would brook no opposition. He did not suffer fools gladly and, in addition to this, from 1944 onward, he suffered from an acute form of diabetes. The illness meant that he suffered from frequent headaches, chronic thirst, and mood swings that are common to the disease.

As the leader of a religious group, Escrivá believed that his job was to ensure that all his flock followed the rules of Opus Dei to the letter. He allegedly set the example in self-mortification — there are unsubstantiated accounts of the walls of his room being splattered with blood after he used the flagellum (a waxed cord-like whip) on himself.

ESCRIVÁ'S CRITICS
Many of Escrivá's most vociferous critics have been Catholics who are worried about Opus Dei's alleged power in the Vatican and ex-members of Opus Dei itself. For example, one of Escrivá's strongest critics is María del Carmen Tapia, an ex-numerary member of Opus Dei, who worked in the secretariat in the Central House in Rome. She has accused him of being vain and prone to

BELOW Josemaría saying the rosary, kneeling with Javier Echevarría and Álvaro del Portillo at the shrine of our Lady of Lujan, in Argentina.

ABOVE Josemaría saying Mass. For him, the Mass was the "centre and root of the interior life".

tantrums, saying that he would berate and ridicule anyone who did not do their work perfectly. She alleges in her book *Beyond the Threshold: A Life in Opus Dei*, that he screamed at her, calling her a whore, a sow, a wicked woman and worthless.

There can be no doubt that Escrivá was a man of contradictions, and it is no wonder that his critics are at pains to point these out. He sang the praises of celibacy in *The Way* (Maxim 28): "Marriage is for the soldiers, not for the General Staff of Christ's Army." However, he also calls marriage a vocation, and in his later book, *Christ Is Passing By,* he wrote: "Christian marriage is not just a social institution, much less a mere remedy for human weakness. It is a real supernatural calling. A great sacrament."

While writing that honours and privileges were "honours, distinctions, titles, things of air, puffs of pride, lies, nothingness", he applied for and accepted an aristocratic title for his family. He also spoke warmly of Jesus and his mother being Jews and included people of all religions as Opus Dei "co-operators" or friends. However, his most vociferous critics have accused him of anti-semitism through supporting fascism and the Nazi regime.

Critics have also lambasted Escrivá for the secrecy within Opus Dei and his fervour over recruiting – in Opus Dei's own magazine, *Crónica*, he wrote: "Holy coercion is necessary, *compelle intrare* the Lord tells us." This is a reference to Jesus' parable in Matthew 22:1-14, which bids guests to a wedding feast.

ESCRIVÁ AND JOHN PAUL II

Pope John Paul II was one of Escrivá's greatest fans, partly because of the Polish pope's own opposition to communism. This is his view of the founder of Opus Dei in a homily given at the time of Escrivá's beatification in 1992: "'I will praise your name for ever, my God and my king.' This acclamation which we sang in the responsorial Psalm is, as it were, the summing up of the spiritual life of Blessed Josemaría. His great love of Christ by whom he is fascinated, impels him to consecrate himself for ever to him and to share in the mystery of his passion and resurrection. He likewise has a filial love for the Virgin Mary which leads him to imitate her virtues. 'I will praise your name for ever': this is the hymn which rose spontaneously in his soul and which led him to offer to God all that was his and all that surrounded him. In fact, his life is marked by Christian humanism, with the unmistakable seal of goodness, meekness of heart, the hidden suffering by which God purifies and sanctifies his chosen ones."

LEFT The Catholic Church had become used to charismatic leaders, shown by the willingness of Pope John Paul II to become more accessible to people worldwide.

SAINTHOOD

JOSEMARÍA ESCRIVÁ COLLAPSED AND DIED IN HIS OFFICE IN ROME ON 26 JUNE 1975 AFTER A VISIT TO THE WOMEN'S COLLEGE OF ST MARY WITH HIS COLLEAGUES, FATHER ÁLVARO DEL PORTILLO AND FATHER JAVIER ECHEVARRÍA. THOUSANDS OF PEOPLE, INCLUDING MANY BISHOPS, REQUESTED THAT THE HOLY SEE INVESTIGATE ESCRIVÁ AS A POTENTIAL CANDIDATE FOR CANONIZATION.

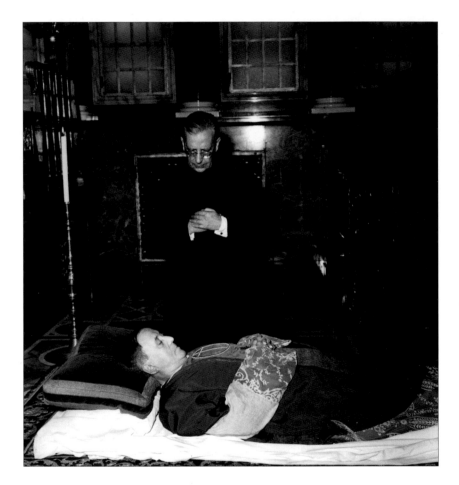

ABOVE Dr Álvaro del Portillo kneeling before the body of Josemaría Escrivá, laid out in Mass vestments in the prelatic church of Our Lady of Peace, Rome. Escrivá asked that no one wear black mourning ties at his funeral, but should instead sing an Italian pop song, *Aprite la finestra al nuovo sole: è primavera* – "Open the windows to the new sun: springtime is here."

Two miracles of healing were attributed to Escrivá after his death – one of the requirements for canonization. The first miracle was the healing of Sister Concepción Boullon Rubio, a 70-year-old nun who had been on the point of death with a tumour as large as an orange, which vanished. The second was the cure of Dr Manuel Nevado Rey, a 60-year-old surgeon, who had untreatable cancerous radiodermatitis that had lasted for 30 years. Escrivá's intercession had been requested via prayer in both cases.

On 17 May 1992, Pope John Paul II beatified Escrivá. He proclaimed him a saint ten years later, on 6 October 2002, in front of more than 300,000 people who overflowed from St Peter's Square up to the Tiber river. The Pope said: "Following in his footsteps, spread in society the awareness that we are called to holiness, without distinction of race, class, culture or age."

FAST-TRACKING

Pope John Paul II was renowned for canonizing more saints than any other pope – a total of 482 – and Escrivá's case moved swiftly through the process of beatification and canonization in just 27 years. Beatification (the intermediate step) took place in just 17 years, a record since the 16th century. Before the 16th century, times between death and canonization were often much shorter. For example, St Francis of Assisi was canonized only four years after his death. John Paul II amended the process in 1983, and since then, Escrivá's record has been broken by the beatification of Mother Teresa of Calcutta in an extraordinary six years.

There is no doubt that the financial support and commitment of Opus Dei contributed to the speed of the canonization. There are many stages to becoming a saint, and much information has to be gathered to complete any investigation. It was incredibly important for Opus Dei to have their founder canonized, and it is not surprising that they rallied round to research and produce the evidence required. Most candidates for beatification and canonization do not receive such a high level of support. Another member of Opus Dei, a Spanish teacher and female numerary, was also recommended as a candidate for beatification in 1975, but the process is still awaiting completion.

OBJECTIONS

The loudest objections to Escrivá's canonization came from ex-members of Opus Dei. Some of the most serious complaints included accusations that critics of Escrivá were prevented from testifying at the church tribunals set up to investigate his life. Opus Dei says that 11 critics were heard among 92 witnesses. However, several prominent former members who had criticized Escrivá publicly did not have a hearing, including María del Carmen Tapia, Father Vladimir Feltzman, who believed that Escrivá had minimized the magnitude of the Holocaust, and John Roche, a former numerary. A group of former members of Opus Dei also wrote to the

Saints are not politically correct people. By everyday standards, they are fanatics, willing to be martyred for their faith and unswerving in their belief. They are not afraid to be controversial and are almost always willing to suffer. St Rose of Lima, for example, was so afraid that her beauty might be a temptation to someone, she rubbed her face with pepper until it was red and blistered. Many saints have been known for their fanatical beliefs, including denouncing all non-Catholics as heretics.

ABOVE St Peter's Square, Rome, during the beatification of Escrivá and Josephine Bakhita, a Sudanese woman kidnapped by slave traders at the age of nine. She lived as a nun with the Canossian Sisterhood in Italy for more than 50 years.

ABOVE St Rose of Lima by Carlo Dolci. As well as rubbing her face with pepper until it was red and blistered, St Rose wore a metal spiked crown concealed by roses, and an iron chain about her waist, and would go for days without food. When she could no longer stand, she lay on a bed, constructed by herself, of broken glass, stone and thorns. She was the first South American to be canonized.

Pope attacking Escrivá for his "arrogance and malevolent temper ... his indifference to the poor, his love of luxury and ostentation". In addition, there were allegations that 40 per cent of the testimony which promoted Escrivá's cause came from just two men: Álvaro del Portillo and Javier Echevarría, both of whom succeeded Escrivá as leaders of Opus Dei.

SUCCESSION

Father del Portillo, a friend and loyal supporter from the first years of Opus Dei in Spain, succeeded Escrivá. When Opus Dei was established as a personal prelature on 28 November 1982, Pope John Paul II appointed Father del Portillo as prelate of Opus Dei. The pope then ordained him as a bishop in 1991. After Bishop del Portillo's death in 1994, Javier Echevarría was appointed prelate and ordained as a bishop by Pope John Paul II the following year.

LEFT A seated portrait of St Bernadette of Lourdes, visionary and messenger of the Immaculate Conception.

PART THREE

OPUS DEI TODAY

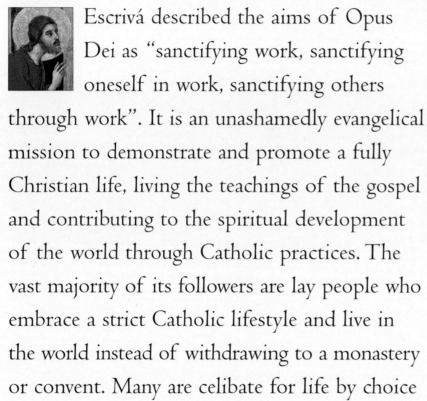Escrivá described the aims of Opus Dei as "sanctifying work, sanctifying oneself in work, sanctifying others through work". It is an unashamedly evangelical mission to demonstrate and promote a fully Christian life, living the teachings of the gospel and contributing to the spiritual development of the world through Catholic practices. The vast majority of its followers are lay people who embrace a strict Catholic lifestyle and live in the world instead of withdrawing to a monastery or convent. Many are celibate for life by choice and make a commitment of fidelity to Opus Dei while holding ordinary jobs. Priests, monks and nuns are easily recognizable through their clothing; members of Opus Dei are not, which may be one of the reasons why they have developed a reputation for secrecy.

RIGHT Christ washing his disciples feet, from the back panels of *La Maesta* (Majesty), painted in 1308 for the high altar of Siena Cathedral, Italy. Escrivá's belief was that everyone could – and should – become an apostle of Christ through their everyday work, whether it was caring for people, cleaning, raising children or running a company.

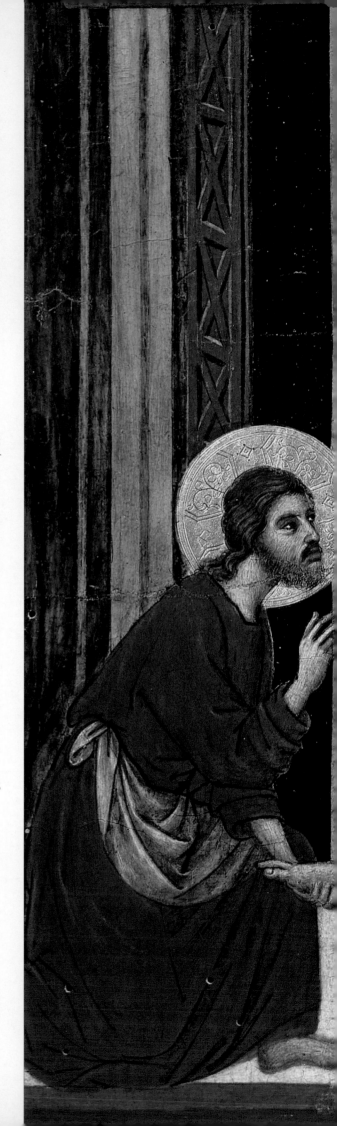

PERSONAL PRELATURE

WHEN OPUS DEI WAS FOUNDED IN 1928, AND FOR THE NEXT TWO DECADES, IT WAS REGARDED AS AN EXTRAORDINARY DEPARTURE FROM ACCEPTED ORTHODOXY IN THE CATHOLIC CHURCH. THIS WAS BECAUSE ESCRIVÁ BELIEVED LAY PEOPLE SHOULD SHARE THE SAME VOCATION AS THE PRIESTHOOD AND BE CONSIDERED EQUAL IN SPIRITUAL WORK. IN THE 1960S, HOWEVER, THE SECOND VATICAN COUNCIL EXPRESSED A WISH BOTH TO EXTEND THE ROLE OF LAY PEOPLE IN THE CHURCH AND TO EVANGELIZE TO THE WORLD. AS A NATURAL PROGRESSION OF THIS IDEA, THE VATICAN DEVELOPED PERSONAL PRELATURES.

RIGHT The present bishop-prelate of Opus Dei, Monsignor Javier Echevarría. On creating the prelature, John Paul II said Escrivá founded it *ductus divina inspiratione*, "led by divine inspiration", an assertion disputed by its critics.

BELOW John Paul II ordaining the first Opus Dei prelate, Bishop Álvaro del Portillo. He served as the prelate of Opus Dei between 1982 and 1994.

The term "personal" means that membership of the organization is not linked to territory as a church diocese is, while "prelature" means that at the head of the organization there is a "prelate", or leader, who is appointed by the pope. However, a personal prelature is not a religious order or an association, and members are still subject to their local bishop and diocese. It is an institution that has its own clergy and may have lay members who carry out specific spiritual duties, but they are not required to take the vows of poverty, chastity and obedience as religious orders do. The prelate will usually be a bishop, and women cannot be prelates.

In 1982, Opus Dei was established as a personal prelature by Pope John Paul II and, so far, is the only personal prelature in existence. St Josemaría Escrivá was never prelate of Opus Dei, as he died before the prelature was granted. The prelate of Opus Dei is currently Bishop Javier Echevarría, who joined in 1948 and worked as secretary to Escrivá for 20 years. The prelate of Opus Dei is the only member who remains in his job for life.

OTHER GROUPS

Opus Dei is not the only Catholic group that includes both priests and lay people, although it was certainly the first. Comunione e Liberazione is an Italian group founded by Father Luigi Guissano in 1954. Like Opus Dei, its members are mostly lay Catholics, including some who are committed to lifelong celibacy. The group does not keep a list of followers, but approximately

100,000 people in Italy attend its meetings, and it has representation in about 70 countries. Regnum Christi is an apostolic movement, founded by Father Marcel Maciel in 1959, that includes lay men and women, as well as deacons and priests. It has about 40,000 members in 60 countries. Members include some adherents of other Christian denominations as well as Catholics.

The Focolare is a broadly similar group but of lay people only and founded by a woman, Chiara Lubich, in Italy during the Second World War. Based on the belief that God is Love, the group is ecumenical and has 87,000 members worldwide. The Focolare has Vatican approval and the right to enrol priests.

The Neocatechumenate movement was founded by Spaniards Francisco Arguello and Carmen Hernández in 1968. It teaches that the Church must return to the example of the early Christians. They have 13,500 communities in 90 countries and more than half their number are lay people. They have been unofficially endorsed by three popes.

WHY IS OPUS DEI SO FAVOURED?

One of the criticisms of Opus Dei is the degree to which it was seen to be favoured by Pope John Paul II and the equal support it is now receiving from his successor, Benedict XVI. There is no doubt that John Paul II was a great admirer of Escrivá. On the one hand, Opus Dei stands for all that is conservative in the Catholic faith. On the other, it invented a completely new form for evangelization of the Church that includes both priests and lay people, which perfectly fulfilled John Paul's project of a "second evangelization" and his passion for the universality of sanctity in the Church. He thought that Opus Dei embodied the charisma that established orders such as the Jesuits, Franciscans and Carmelites formerly had. Also, these institutions are exclusively for priests, monks or nuns and do not include lay people.

IMPORTANCE OF THE PRELATURE

As a qualified lawyer, Escrivá was renowned for ensuring that all appropriate canonical and juridical fine print was fully examined. Opus Dei has gone through the differing forms of being a Pious Union, the Priestly Society of the Holy Cross, a secular institute and finally a personal prelature. All these roles were intended, by Escrivá, to protect it and, in a way, to define the indefinable. Without a structure that was recognized within the Church, Opus Dei would not be able to operate as it does, with both lay and women members.

There is no simple way to define Opus Dei apart from saying that it is a personal prelature. Without being a prelature, Opus Dei would always be in danger of being sidelined into other departments within canon law – either as a religious order, where there could be no lay people, or as a lay association, which would not cater for priests and would also not have a structure for a celibate vocation.

ABOVE A meeting of Pope John XXIII's ecumenical council in St Peter's Basilica, Vatican City, popularly known as the Second Vatican Council.

BELOW A statue of Josemaría Escrivá in the courtyard of the Opus Dei-run University of Navarra in Spain.

GLOBAL ORGANIZATION

OPUS DEI IS RUN BY THE PRELATURE IN A COLLEGIAL STYLE, MEANING THAT THE PRELATE DOES NOT GOVERN OR MAKE DECISIONS ON HIS OWN BUT ALWAYS WITH THE AGREEMENT OF VARIOUS COUNCILS. THE COUNCILS ARE BASED IN ROME AND MADE UP LARGELY OF LAITY. THE COUNCIL FOR WOMEN IS CALLED THE CENTRAL ADVISORY, AND THE COUNCIL FOR MEN IS KNOWN AS THE GENERAL COUNCIL.

RIGHT Opus Dei's head office in Rome is a vital nerve centre for the prelature worldwide. This photo is taken from the Via di Villa Sacchetti, a side entrance to the building that sits on Viale Bruno Buozzi. The building contains 24 chapels.

BELOW Residents on the men's terrace at Netherhall House, an intercollegiate hall of residence in Hampstead, London, in the UK, which marked its 50th anniversary in 2002. Women in Netherhall House live in an entirely separate area.

Opus Dei is divided into regions, each one having a regional vicar and two councils: a Regional Advisory for women and a Regional Commission for men. The same collegial style applies in each country, so the regional vicar of a country will always make decisions in consensus with his country's councils. Some of the larger regions are subdivided into delegations, which have the same governmental organization: a vicar of the delegation and two councils. Finally, at the local level, there are Opus Dei centres, which are responsible for organizing spiritual development and pastoral care for the area. Centres may be for women or for men but not both, and each one is governed by a local council, which is headed by a lay person (the director). Each one has pastoral care from an Opus Dei priest. Opus Dei now has centres in 62 countries and co-operators and individual members in many more.

THE UNITED STATES

Opus Dei opened its doors in the USA in Chicago in 1949, and it now has 3,000 members countrywide. Its activities are organized in 60 centres in 19 cities, which include Boston, Chicago, Dallas, Houston, Los Angeles, New York, San Francisco and Washington DC. Opus Dei's headquarters in the USA are in a $47 million, 133,000-square-foot purpose-built centre on Lexington Avenue, New York City, made possible by donations. The building incorporates seven chapels and sacristies and six dining rooms with separate sections. There are entrances on different streets for the men and women of Opus Dei, although anyone visiting the centre can enter either section, whatever their gender.

Opus Dei also sponsors an education programme for children in the South Bronx, and other educational initiatives are run in Syracuse, Philadelphia, Miami, San Antonio, Minneapolis/St Paul, Denver and Phoenix. The prelature's corporate works include five

high schools in the USA: The Heights (for boys) and Oak Crest (for girls) in Washington DC, the Montrose School (for girls) in Boston, and Northridge Prep (for boys) and The Willows (for girls) in Chicago. Their retreat houses include the Fetherock Conference Center near Houston, Texas, and Trumbull Manor near San Francisco, California.

SPAIN

As the founding country of Opus Dei, Spain will always be close to members' hearts, although the prelature has not always thrived there over the last 50 years. The shrine of Our Lady at Torreciudad, in Aragon, where Escrivá's mother took him in gratitude for his recovery from illness, is not the Spanish headquarters of Opus Dei, but it is a spiritual heartland for the prelature, and many retreats and ordinations are carried out there. Devotion to Our Lady of Torreciudad dates back to the 11th century and the restored shrine was inaugurated on 7 July 1975. Opus Dei runs IESE, one of the nation's leading business schools, and the University of Navarra, which Escrivá founded in 1952.

ITALY

The prelature of Opus Dei is international, but its central offices are in Rome. The central Church of the prelature is the Oratory of Our Lady of Peace in Viale Bruno Buozzi, where Escrivá's body is buried. The prelature's main communications and press office is in Rome. The Prelatic Curia has its offices at Viale Bruno Buozzi, and there are three public churches entrusted to Opus Dei in Rome. Members often travel to Rome to attend courses or retreats there.

UNITED KINGDOM

The headquarters of Opus Dei in the UK are at Orme Court, a terrace of houses in Bayswater, London, now made famous by Dan Brown's novel

The Da Vinci Code. The prelature set up office in the UK in 1946 and now has 25 centres in and around London, Oxford, Manchester and Glasgow. The first corporate work in the UK was Netherhall House, an intercollegiate university residence in Hampstead, London, which opened in 1952. Other student residences in Britain are Ashwell House for women in Islington, London, Greygarth Hall and Coniston Hall in Manchester, and Grandpont House and Winton in Oxford. There are two conference centres: Wickenden Manor in West Sussex and Thornycroft Hall in Cheshire. There are three hospitality training centres for women: two in London and one in Manchester. There are also educational and social activities in inner-city areas of London, Manchester and Glasgow.

ABOVE The Shrine of Our Lady of Torreciudad is one of the most visited places in the Aragon Pyrenees. Thousands of people come to the pilgrimage centre each year. The inaugural Mass (on 7 July 1975) was, in fact, a funeral Mass for Josemaría Escrivá, who had died 11 days earlier.

BELOW Bishop Javier Echevarría, Monsignors Fernando Ocáriz and Joaquín Alonso at the crypt chapel of the Our Lady of Peace church in Rome, where Josemaría Escrivá was buried on 27 June 1975. Under the Opus Dei seal on the tombstone are the words "El Padre" (The Father) and below it, the date of his birth 9-I-1902, and that of his death 26-VI-75.

MEMBERS OF OPUS DEI

OPUS DEI NOW HAS APPROXIMATELY 85,500 MEMBERS WORLDWIDE AND CENTRES IN 62 COUNTRIES, THE LATEST BEING KAZAKHSTAN, SOUTH AFRICA, SLOVENIA, CROATIA AND LITHUANIA. SPAIN HAS THE LARGEST PROPORTION OF MEMBERS, FOLLOWED BY MEXICO, ARGENTINA, ITALY, THE USA, COLOMBIA AND THE PHILIPPINES. GIVEN THAT THE FOUNDING COUNTRY WAS SPAIN, IT IS NO SURPRISE THAT OPUS DEI IS PARTICULARLY POPULAR WITH CATHOLIC HISPANIC CULTURES. GREAT BRITAIN WAS ONE OF THE FIRST THREE COUNTRIES OUTSIDE SPAIN WHERE OPUS DEI FOUND A FOOTING IN 1946. ESCRIVÁ SPENT FIVE SUMMERS IN ENGLAND IN THE 1950S, CALLING IT A CROSSROADS OF THE WORLD.

ABOVE An American university graduation ceremony. Opus Dei is frequently accused of targeting socially advantaged, intelligent young people to become members. The exacting requirements of Opus Dei membership would appear to attract those who are already driven to be perfectionists.

RIGHT Opus Dei's dedication of life and work to the service of God, and its strong work ethic, ensure that members who are happy in the prelature are committed to succeeding in whatever venture they undertake.

By far the highest concentration of Opus Dei membership is in Europe, with 49,000 followers. The Americas come second with 29,400 members, followed by Asia and the Pacific with 4,800 and Africa with 1,800.

Spain, the founding country, has 24,000 members, 5,000 of whom are numeraries. The USA has 3,000 members. Britain has about 500 members, which is very few when one takes into account how long Opus Dei has been established there. On average, fewer than a dozen new people join in Britain each year. This may be because the late Cardinal Basil Hume, Archbishop of Westminster, expressed reservations about Opus Dei. Moreover, the proportion of Catholics

in the country is far lower there than in many other countries. In Spain, 98 per cent of the population is Catholic, in Italy 96 per cent and in France 62 per cent, whereas in England and Wales the proportion is just 8 per cent. The Americas are home to nearly half the world's baptized Catholics (49.8 per cent according to British Broadcasting Corporation statistics), but most of them live in Latin and South America. Only 20 per cent of the population of the US is Catholic. That Europe has a higher percentage of Opus Dei members than the Americas may be due to the high proportion of members in its founding country, Spain, or it could be, as detractors of Opus Dei would claim, due to it being a group that focuses on recruitment among the affluent classes.

ORDINARY PEOPLE

On the whole, Opus Dei members are ordinary people with an extraordinary lifestyle. Opus Dei members come from all walks of life, from poets, bus drivers, teachers, hairdressers, accountants through to scientists and business people. What they all have in common is that they dedicate their work to God every moment of every day. Often the prelature is criticized for targeting university graduates as new recruits, so it is at pains to point out that most of its members are everyday people, including disabled people who are unable to hold full-time jobs. More importantly, the membership is comprised of people who are orthodox Catholics, who have received a vocation (calling) to join and who are prepared to submit themselves to the intense discipline and internal spiritual focus that is an integral part of Opus Dei.

MIXING WITH OTHERS

Nowadays it is quite simple for Opus Dei members in some countries to send their children to an Opus Dei school and college, to spend all their spare time in Opus Dei activities and for most of their friends to be in Opus Dei. While this may be comfortable, it is not fulfilling the creed of the prelature to live the work in the world, offering an example to others. It may also, unwittingly, be fuelling the parallel beliefs about the prelature that it is secretive and that it is unduly powerful. Opus Dei aims to be a worldwide family where members are committed to helping each other spiritually. Escrivá specifically forbade members to help each other materially, so that the prelature could never be accused of being a mutual help society.

OPUS DEI SAINTS

There is just one saint in Opus Dei – the founder, St Josemaría Escrivá. However, it may well have several more in the coming decades. In 2001, the process of beatification began for Guadalupe Ortíz de Landázuri of Madrid, a laywoman member of Opus Dei and a high school teacher, who died in 1975. She was one of the first women to join Opus Dei and worked for six years in Mexico, educating young women in rural communities.

Other current candidates for beatification are Isidoro Zorzano, an Argentinian-born civil engineer who was one of Opus Dei's very first members in Spain; Bishop Álvaro del Portillo, first prelate of Opus Dei; Toni Zweifel, a Swiss engineer; and Montserrat Grases, a student who died of cancer at the age of 17.

LEFT Any or all of these people could be members of Opus Dei. Just like any secular church organization, members are encouraged to live life in the world. Even numeraries and associates, the Opus Dei celibates, work in jobs outside the centres where they live.

BELOW Opus Dei members are not all university graduates or active in politics or the corporate world. Many members work as bus drivers, hairdressers and in other low-paid jobs. However, they all have one thing in common – they do their job to the best of their ability and offer that service to God.

COUNTRIES WITH OPUS DEI MEMBERS

Opus Dei now has centres in 62 countries and co-operators and individual members in many more. The countries where centres are based are: Portugal, Italy, Great Britain, France, Ireland, Mexico, the USA, Chile, Argentina, Colombia, Venezuela, Germany, Guatemala, Peru, Ecuador, Uruguay, Switzerland, Brazil, Austria, Canada, Japan, Kenya, El Salvador, Costa Rica, Holland, Paraguay, Australia, the Philippines, Belgium, Nigeria, Puerto Rico, Bolivia, Congo, Ivory Coast, Honduras, Hong Kong, Singapore, Trinidad and Tobago, Sweden, Taiwan, Finland, Cameroon, the Dominican Republic, Macao, New Zealand, Poland, Hungary, the Czech Republic, Nicaragua, India, Israel, Lithuania, Estonia, Slovakia, Lebanon, Panama, Uganda, Kazakhstan, South Africa, Croatia, Slovenia and Latvia.

INFLUENCE AND POWER

FOR A GROUP WITH FEWER MEMBERS THAN WOULD FILL A PREMIER DIVISION FOOTBALL STADIUM ON A SATURDAY AFTERNOON, OPUS DEI'S REACH IS WIDE AND, AS IT IS CONCERNED WITH SPIRITUAL DEVELOPMENT, IT IS MOSTLY INVISIBLE TO THE SECULAR WORLD. MEMBERS HAVE BEEN STRONGLY INFLUENTIAL WITHIN THE CATHOLIC CHURCH, AND OPUS DEI ENJOYED GREAT FAVOUR WITH POPE JOHN PAUL II. ONE OF THE MAIN AUTHORS OF *DOMINUS IESUS*, THE POPE'S 2001 DOCUMENT THAT STATED THAT ALL RELIGIONS OTHER THAN CHRISTIANITY WERE "GRAVELY DEFICIENT", WAS MONSIGNOR FERNANDO OCÁRIZ, VICAR-GENERAL OF OPUS DEI.

Gutiérrez Gómez, an official in the Congregation for the Causes of Saints; and Father Miguel Delgado, *capo ufficio* in the Pontifical Council for the Laity.

Members of the Priestly Society of the Holy Cross (Opus Dei priests) in the Vatican include: Bishop Justo Mullor, president of the Accademia Ecclesiastica; Monsignor Nguyen Van Phuong, a *capo ufficio* in the Congregation for the Evangelization of Peoples; Monsignor Jacques Suaudeau, an official of the Pontifical Academy for Life; Father Andrew Baker, an official in the Congregation for Bishops; and Father Gregory Gaston, an official in the Pontifical Council for the Family.

ABOVE The temptation of St Anthony of Egypt, founder of monasticism. St Anthony followed the lead of an Egyptian sect called the Therapeutae who lived a life of self-denial in the desert. He reputedly healed skin conditions and lived to a great age.

RIGHT Spanish Cardinal Herranz at a press conference at the Vatican in February 2005. The Vatican had just issued the first revised guidebook on marriage annulments in nearly 70 years, called *Dignitatis Connubii* (The Dignity of Marriage).

Power is transitory in modern democratic societies, but since the Second World War, many of the Hispanic governments of the world have contained Opus Dei members. In the Vatican, where positions of power are frequently held for life, over the last decade, an average of 20 out of a total of 2,659 employees have been members of Opus Dei. Long-term Opus Dei Vatican employees include: Cardinal Julian Herranz, President of the Pontifical Council for the Interpretation of Legislative Texts; Monsignor Francesco Di Muzio, a *capo ufficio*, or mid-level manager, in the Congregation for the Evangelization of Peoples; Monsignor José Luis

CONTROVERSY

At the opposite end of the scale is American former supernumerary Robert Hanssen, who worked for the FBI and was convicted of spying for both the USSR and Russia. He was charged with selling American secrets over a period of 15 years in return for a reported $1.4 million in cash and diamonds. Hanssen pleaded guilty to charges of espionage and conspiracy in exchange for federal prosecutors agreeing not to seek the death penalty. He was sentenced to life in prison without parole in 2001 and resigned his membership of Opus Dei after his conviction.

OPUS DEI AND POLITICS

In the 1982 decree that established Opus Dei as a personal prelature, it is specified that Opus Dei has no political or business agenda: directors of centres, spiritual directors and the prelate himself, are responsible only for the spiritual health of their flock. However, members of Opus Dei have uniform views on faith, morality and ethics, so any member of the prelature with any influence will support the Catholic political line when it is relevant such as on issues of contraception and abortion, homosexuality, cloning or divorce. Given the Opus Dei work ethic, any member involved with politics will probably go the extra mile to be more influential than a less motivated colleague.

Opus Dei's website states: "Members can be involved in any honest activity they choose to be engaged in. Many will have little or no interest in party politics, although some of course will. If they do play a role, they do so without in any way representing Opus Dei but as free and responsible individuals, following their own lights and answering in exactly the same way and to exactly the same people as anyone else."

Escrivá himself wrote in his book *Christ Is Passing By*: "I never talk politics. I do not approve of committed Christians in the world forming a political-religious movement."

LEFT Robert Hanssen was a 27-year veteran with the US Federal Bureau of Investigation. Hanssen confessed to Reverend Bucciarelli, former head of Opus Dei in the US. The confession and advice is privileged and the priest kept his vow of confidentiality. The spying had continued for years afterwards.

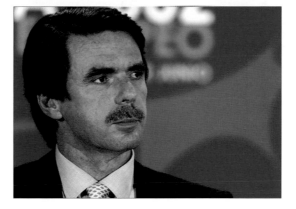

LEFT Former Prime Minister of Spain, José María Aznar, whose government contained several Opus Dei dignitaries. Aznar sent two of his children to Opus Dei-run schools.

In his book *Opus Dei: Secrets and Power Inside the Catholic Church*, John Allen points out that in 1970s and 80s Peru, numerary members Rafael Rey and Rodrigo Franco Montes were members of opposing political parties, yet lived together in the same Opus Dei centre. He also remarks that in Spain, numerary Pilar Urbano, a journalist, attacked supernumerary Federic Trillio's position on supporting the Iraq war as being dishonest.

RUTH KELLY – YOUNGEST BRITISH CABINET MEMBER

One of the more high-profile British members of Opus Dei is the MP Ruth Kelly. At the age of 36, Ruth was the youngest woman to sit in the British Cabinet. She was appointed Education Secretary in the Labour government in 2004 and was made secretary of a brand new department – Community and Local Government – in 2006. Both Ruth and her brother Dr Ronan Kelly are supernumeraries. Ruth Kelly has responsibility for a £1 billion research budget. She opposed motions on embryo research in Parliament and is reported to have told Prime Minister Tony Blair that she could never support stem-cell research.

MEMBERSHIP STRUCTURE

OPUS DEI'S STRUCTURAL POWER BASE IS SITUATED IN ROME WITH THE PRELATE AS OVERALL LEADER. HOWEVER, THE PRELATURE IS INTENDED TO BE AS UNSTRUCTURED AS POSSIBLE – ESCRIVÁ CALLED IT "A DISORGANIZED ORGANIZATION" – AND NO MEMBER OF OPUS DEI IS REGARDED AS BEING GREATER OR LESSER THAN THE OTHERS. OPUS DEI MEMBERS ARE DIVIDED INTO FIVE CATEGORIES, WHICH HAVE NAMES BASED ON TRADITIONAL SPANISH TERMS FOR DIFFERENT CATEGORIES OF UNIVERSITY PROFESSORS.

RIGHT Father Gerard Sheehan, parish priest of St Thomas More church in London, which has a congregation of 500. Opus Dei was given the church in 2005, its first parish in Great Britain since it was founded in 1928. Father Sheehan is one of 17 Opus Dei priests in Britain.

BELOW John Perrotet, his wife, Anne, and their 12 children, from Sydney, Australia. The couple are committed members of the prelature. John says: "Having a large family is certainly hard work, but it is immeasurably rewarding and can be lots of fun."

The only distinguishing criterion that is made is how much time each member has available for Opus Dei activities. A full-time employed doctor with four children and a working husband would not be expected to give as much time as a celibate person living within an Opus Dei community.

PRIESTS

Opus Dei has 1,850 priests and their primary work is to undertake pastoral care of other Opus Dei members. In addition to being a personal prelature, Opus Dei also incorporates The Priestly Society of The Holy Cross. This is an association for the priests of Opus Dei and any diocesan priests who might wish to join in with their particular spirituality but who would not come under the jurisdiction of the prelate. Each diocesan priest continues to work with his own diocese and depends solely on his own bishop, to whom he gives an account of his pastoral work.

SUPERNUMERARIES

About 70 per cent of Opus Dei members are supernumeraries, people who live in the world, in their own homes, and have their own jobs. Supernumeraries are generally married, though it is not required, and many of them are married to someone who is not a member of Opus Dei. They are expected to contribute financially to Opus Dei, but their own family needs must be taken care of first. Supernumeraries are regarded as being "where the action is", with perhaps the greatest spiritual task of sanctifying life and work while doing the school run, working in a secular workplace, and dealing with family. As deeply observant Catholics, supernumerary couples often have higher than average numbers of children.

NUMERARIES

About 20 per cent of Opus Dei members are numeraries, but they get the lion's share of interest from the press and public. Numeraries make a commitment to celibacy and live in an Opus Dei centre with members of their own sex only. Most have an outside job, but what money they can spare from personal expenses goes to Opus Dei, and their family *is* Opus Dei. Only numeraries can be directors of Opus Dei centres, and many of them act as spiritual directors. A vital segment of the numeraries are the assistant numeraries, who are always women. They take care of the homes in which other numeraries live, and their duties include cooking and cleaning.

ASSOCIATES

Associates are unlike numeraries in that they live outside of the centre – although they too are celibate members of Opus Dei. A man or woman who has an elderly parent or who has been widowed and left with children to care for might feel the vocation to join but would become an associate rather than leaving the family to fend

for itself. People with highly demanding jobs, such as a fire-fighter or a doctor, might also choose to be a celibate associate so that they would not have the extra commitment to a spouse or children that might impede them from being more available for their work.

CO-OPERATORS

More than 50 per cent of Opus Dei's 165,000 co-operators are women: friends of Opus Dei who offer their support through prayer and financial donations, and who attend groups and lectures when they wish to do so. They can be of any religion whatsoever, and today Opus Dei has co-operators who are Jewish, Muslim and Buddhist. This was a new departure for the Catholic Church in 1950, when the Vatican ruled that Opus Dei had the right to enrol non-Catholics.

ABOVE One of the 150 staff who work at the Opus Dei-run University of Navarra's Department of Medicine Clinic in Spain. The clinic receives on average 13,000 patients each year.

LEFT *Praying Woman, Golden Sky*, by Yuri Goul. Women's spirituality saw a great resurgence in the 20th century with the advent of women priests and rabbis in some sections of Christianity and Judaism. Many Catholic women see nothing wrong with having only male clergy, while simultaneously focusing directly on their own spirituality.

THE ROLE OF WOMEN

One of the most common criticisms of Opus Dei is of its "archaic" attitude towards women. This does not stem from the fact that Opus Dei women cannot be priests (which is the case for the entire Catholic Church) but from the position of assistant numeraries. In the 21st century, the idea of only women doing "menial work" is offensive to many people. This is exacerbated by the fact that women act as housekeepers for male numeraries as well as for female ones. The ethos of Opus Dei is to sanctify work, and the organization claims that assistant numeraries choose to commit their lives to being housekeepers as a vocation. Assistant numeraries receive exactly the same level of spiritual teaching and guidance as every other member of Opus Dei.

SPIRITUAL LIFESTYLE

MEMBERS OF OPUS DEI BELIEVE THAT HOLINESS IS NOT JUST FOR PRIESTS AND NOT ONLY ACHIEVED THROUGH THE PRACTICE OF CONTEMPLATION AND PRAYER, BUT IS TO BE EXPERIENCED THROUGH EVERYDAY ACTIVITIES FROM WASHING UP AND GARDENING TO THE MOST INTRICATE WORK OF AN ENGINEER OR THE MINISTRATIONS OF A DOCTOR OR NURSE.

RIGHT A woman in the pews in the women's chapel at the New York headquarters of Opus Dei. All centres have their own private oratories for the men or women who live there. Private devotion and solitary prayer is a vital part of the life of each Opus Dei member, as well as attending daily Mass with others.

BELOW A Filipino painting of Escrivá surrounded by people sanctifying their work. Commissioned to commemorate the birth centenary of Josemaría in 2002 (he was born on 2 January 1902), the image was used on one of the national postage stamps circulated in the Philippines that year.

Escrivá taught that the real "action" of holiness is in the world, where decisions have to be made every moment, rather than in prayer, and where there is time to recollect and consider.

Making every moment sacred is a lifetime's vocation, and members of Opus Dei admit that it is both hard and often unachievable. However, the idea is to attempt it at all times and not to be discouraged by failure. The idea of total attention to the sanctification of work does not necessarily make Opus Dei people popular in the workplace. Perfectionists can be hard taskmasters or difficult work colleagues, especially when they adhere to a strong religious faith. Opus Dei members will have a crucifix or a picture of the Virgin Mary over their desk and are unlikely to join in with office gossip or to take "a sickie". For them, every aspect of the daily routine is an offering to God and must be as perfect as possible.

LIVING AS A SAINT

Opus Dei believes that every human being is called to become an apostle of Christ and a saint. There can be some misinterpretation about the role of the Opus Dei saint, particularly given the publicity that the canonization of their founder, Escrivá, received in 2002. The aim is not to become famous or acknowledged but to serve God quietly. Escrivá taught that Jesus Christ did not take up the mantle of Messiah when he began his public ministry. He did so in the years before his baptism, when he worked as a carpenter in his earthly father's workshop.

Living as a saint also means giving up luxuries and comforts and following an ascetic lifestyle that includes making some kind of sacrifice. For Opus Dei members the level of asceticism appears to be a balance between the views of the director who runs the centre to which they are affiliated

49

SPIRITUAL LIFESTYLE

and personal choice. All Opus Dei members are expected to practise psychological self-mortification through the denial of treats such as a second helping of supper, a cup of coffee or a comfortable seat. Guidelines for numeraries, assistant numeraries and associates include corporal self-mortification and a higher level of psychological self-mortification. How testing these may be will often depend upon the practices of a specific centre.

SPIRITUAL PRACTICE

Every member of Opus Dei is expected to carry out what are called "the norms" on a daily basis. This daily routine includes a morning prayer, which dedicates the day to God, going to Mass, two sessions of up to half an hour of prayer a day, several other forms of prayer, including the rosary, and a set of prayers in Latin called the "Preces", a daily examination of conscience, and at least ten minutes of reading or meditating on spiritual literature. According to where the Opus Dei member lives, these routines may be performed alone or together and at times that are appropriate.

All members receive training, support and advice known as "spiritual formation". There is also a weekly "circle" where a member of the group leads a class on some aspect of life in Opus Dei, and a monthly day or evening of recollection, which includes meditation led by a priest, a talk, and time for silent prayer. At least once a year, all members will attend a workshop on the spiritual life, the length of which varies from three days to three weeks according to the vocation of the member. Finally, all members of Opus Dei are expected to attend an annual retreat of several days spent in silence and meditation.

FREEDOM AND CONTROL

Members of Opus Dei must have unswerving loyalty to Escrivá and his teachings and be willing to show complete obedience to the rulings of their superiors, should they be asked to do so. In some centres the rules are applied more vigorously than in others. Paradoxically, this individual interpretation of the Opus Dei lifestyle reflects both freedom and control and is one of the more controversial characteristics of Opus Dei. Some ex-members, including Dr John Roche, a former numerary in Galway, Ireland, claim that permission must be sought before leaving the house, watching any television or reading any books apart from Escrivá's writings or the Bible. However, John Allen, the Vatican correspondent for the *National Catholic Reporter* and author of *Opus Dei: Secrets and Power Inside the Catholic Church*, reports seeing male numeraries excitedly planning to watch a football match on the television.

SPIRITUAL DIRECTION

All members of Opus Dei receive spiritual direction from a fellow member at least once a fortnight. This is an ancient Christian practice in which one person speaks of his or her life and prayer to a colleague, and both assess how that person can move closer to "a relationship with God". Unlike counselling or therapy, the process is entirely prayer-centred. Unlike confession, which is an examination of sin, it is an exploration of how to develop spiritually. Spiritual directors do not "buddy-up" with each other. A spiritual director is assigned by senior members and is usually a numerary or an associate member.

ABOVE Time off – Opus Dei men participate in a retreat. Times of contemplation and the sharing of experiences are the same to Opus Dei numeraries as a holiday is to the rest of the world. Retreats are intended to refresh the soul and inspire participants to devote themselves anew and refreshed to their spiritual path.

BELOW St Clare of Assisi, who founded the monastic order of Poor Clares at San Damiano, Italy. She led a life of total seclusion and poverty. When she died at the age of 59, Pope Gregory IX came with his court to her funeral.

SELF-MORTIFICATION

THE ABIDING IMAGE OF OPUS DEI FOR READERS OF THE BOOK *THE DA VINCI CODE* MAY BE THE ONE OF SILAS THE MONK BEATING HIMSELF WITH A WHIP UNTIL HE BLED. THE FACT THAT OPUS DEI NUMERARIES USE A "DISCIPLINE", A KIND OF KNOTTED CORD, AND A CILICE, OR BARBED CHAIN AROUND THE LEG, IS GOOD MATERIAL FOR THOSE WHO FIND SUCH PRACTICES DISTASTEFUL. HOWEVER, CORPORAL MORTIFICATION, AS IT IS KNOWN, IS NOTHING NEW IN THE CATHOLIC CHURCH. POPE PAUL VI WORE A HAIR SHIRT UNDER HIS VESTMENTS, AND ST THOMAS MORE, ST IGNATIUS OF LOYOLA, ST JEROME, MOTHER TERESA OF CALCUTTA AND ESCRIVÁ ALL USED THE DISCIPLINE.

RIGHT A discipline – a small, hand-woven cord-like whip approximately 30cm (12in) long – used by Opus Dei numeraries and numerary assistants for self-flagellation while they say a short vocal prayer. Unlike Escrivá and the albino Silas in *The Da Vinci Code*, modern-day members are discouraged from hitting themselves so hard that they draw blood.

It is a little known fact that the Catholic Church advises people to practise mortification. The crucifixion of Jesus Christ demonstrates that voluntary sacrifice has great spiritual value, especially in helping people to resist temptations that lead to sin. Pope John Paul II wrote an apostolic letter on the supernatural value of human suffering, in which he said: "Each man, in his suffering, can also become a sharer in the

RIGHT The sufferings of Christ are the inspiration for the self-denial of saints and Catholics who wish to live a holy life. Once, when an Opus Dei member asked Escrivá why there was an empty cross outside an oratory, he replied, "It is waiting for you." Crucifixes can be found in most Christian churches, but some modern groups prefer to focus on the miracle of Christ's resurrection rather than on his suffering.

redemptive suffering of Christ." According to *Time* magazine, John Paul II did not wear a hair shirt but he offered his physical sufferings up to God, both after the assassination attempt and in later years as his health began to fail. In the New Testament, St Paul wrote: "For if you live according to the flesh you will die, but if by the Spirit you put to death the deeds of the body you will live." (Romans 8:13)

SACRIFICES AND DENIAL
Self-mortification in Opus Dei is most frequently undertaken with small sacrifices such as refraining from having a cup of coffee after a meal, or

declining a bar of chocolate. Many Christians practise some similar sort of act during Lent as a build-up to Easter rather than all year round. Opus Dei also encourages such sacrifices as smiling at someone who is being very irritating,

THE CILICE

A modern-day version of a hair shirt, the cilice (pronounced "sill-is") derives from the Latin word *cilicium*, meaning a covering made of goat's hair from Cilicia, in Asia Minor. Nowadays, a cilice is a spiked chain that numeraries (in common with many branches of religious orders) wear around the top of a thigh for approximately two hours a day, except for Sundays and Church festival days. Correctly used, a cilice does not break the skin but it irritates it and focuses the wearer on overcoming bodily weakness. In *The Da Vinci Code*, Silas winches his cilice so tightly that it punctures the skin. This would be regarded both as ridiculous and as an unhealthy practice by anyone who knows the true purpose of the cilice.

going the extra mile at work to help someone, or giving up a personal comfort that is dear to you. Rumours abound that numeraries must have a daily cold shower; it was the practice of the founder to do so and many Opus Dei members follow his custom, though they are certainly not obliged to do so.

Numeraries of both sexes, under the age of 45, are expected to sleep on the floor or on a board and to sleep without pillows once a week. Getting up on time in the morning, making the bed, doing your duty with perfection, using your time well, regular physical exercise and personal discipline are all regarded as mortification.

SELF-MORTIFICATION AND FASTING

Escrivá frequently used the discipline on himself, and apocryphal but frequently repeated stories tell of his whipping himself until he bled.

Numeraries are expected to use the discipline once a week on their backs or buttocks and to get permission from a spiritual director if they wish to do more. This seeking of permission is seen to be important as it is known that more extreme practices that inflict pain can lead both to pride and an unhealthy attitude towards the body, which are both contrary to spiritual development. Some ex-numeraries have claimed that they were encouraged to use the discipline to a greater extent than was appropriate for them, with negative results.

Fasting is also regarded as mortification, and it is a recognized practice of many religious people. Jews, in particular, have seven fast days each year, one of which is only undertaken by the firstborn male of a family. The best-known Jewish fast day is Yom Kippur, the Day of Atonement. Nowadays, the Catholic Church recommends either fasting or abstinence on Ash Wednesday, every Friday of Lent, Good Friday, Holy Saturday and 24 December (although abstinence on Christmas Eve is no longer followed in the Western world).

LEFT Nearly all the early saints were martyrs – people who chose to be killed through tortures such as stoning, crucifixion, or being eaten by lions, rather than renounce their belief in Christianity. The first Christian martyr was St Stephen, who was stoned to death for his faith (although he is usually depicted as having been shot with arrows). The idea of suffering for faith is integral to the life of a potential saint.

BELOW A cilice, a small, spiked hand-crafted chain worn around the upper thigh by Opus Dei numeraries and assistant numeraries on most days (except Sundays and feast days). It is worn for no longer than two hours at a time and serves to keep the wearer conscious rather than losing focus on the day and its work. The cilice should be uncomfortable but should not bite into the flesh so as to draw blood.

SUPERNUMERARIES

SUPERNUMERARIES CONSTITUTE BY FAR THE LARGEST PROPORTION OF OPUS DEI'S MEMBERSHIP, AND THEY ARE FREQUENTLY AS DEVOTED TO THEIR OWN CHURCH AND DIOCESE AS THEY ARE TO OPUS DEI. THEY ARE USUALLY MARRIED, AND ARE MEN AND WOMEN WHOSE PRINCIPAL VOCATION IS TO SANCTIFY THEIR WORK AND THEIR FAMILY LIFE TOGETHER.

A number of women supernumeraries have held positions of influence in the world, holding down cabinet jobs in government as well as having large families. Female Opus Dei supernumeraries have been cabinet ministers in Italy, Germany and the UK and are also well known for tireless voluntary and charity work.

As Opus Dei is an orthodox Catholic group, supernumeraries do not practise any form of conventional birth control, apart from the "natural family planning" method of abstaining from sex during fertile times. Consequently, Opus Dei women may have as many as six children, as well as holding down full-time jobs.

ABOVE Spirituality in family life is central to Opus Dei principles, and supernumeraries attempt to live a holy life at all times. Families are raised with regular prayer and very high standards of Catholic morality.

RIGHT The principle of the Sacred Mother is integral to the life of a supernumerary woman. In common with all orthodox Catholicism, birth control is forbidden and large families are common. In addition to this, women frequently have high-flying careers.

A look at the conferences organized by Opus Dei members worldwide demonstrates the importance of supernumeraries to the prelature, especially with outreach and evangelism. There is a prevalence of titles such as "Marriage and the family – a path to sanctity", and "Family: a revolution for the third millennium." Escrivá wrote in *Christ Is Passing By*: "Husband and wife are called to sanctify their married life and to sanctify themselves in it. It would be a serious mistake if they were to exclude family life from their spiritual development. The marriage union, the care and education of children, the effort to provide for the needs of the family as well as for its security and development, the relationships with other persons who make up the community, all these are among the ordinary human situations that Christian couples are called upon to sanctify."

work colleagues about their inner life for fear of being thought "holier-than-thou". However, this reticence is often viewed as secrecy by the outside world, which may consider it threatening. Many supernumeraries get up early in the morning to go to Mass before work, but this is not necessarily expected of them. They also practise mortification such as denying themselves simple pleasures in life but do not use the discipline or cilice.

FINANCIAL CONTRIBUTIONS

Like the numeraries, supernumeraries contribute whatever they can to support Opus Dei, but they are expected to take care of their family needs and bills first. Many members give differing amounts each month after assessing what needs to be bought, repaired or serviced. Often it is the supernumeraries who are at the forefront of fund-raising for Opus Dei charitable and educational initiatives through traditional methods, including running a stall at a local school fair, or selling possessions that are no longer required on the eBay website.

MARRIAGE TO AN UNBELIEVER

It is not required for a supernumerary to be married to another supernumerary but, as in all religions, it is thought preferable to be married to someone of the same faith, if not the same denomination. Just like other Opus Dei members, supernumeraries are expected to evangelize and they are also expected to be regular attendees and supporters of their local church. However, tolerance of other faiths makes such a marriage possible, if not completely desirable.

However, supernumerary women who do stay at home to look after children are equally valued within Opus Dei. A married couple's first apostolate (calling) is to their family, especially raising their children in the Christian life and also teaching them to make each moment sacred.

WORK AND FAITH BALANCE

How a supernumerary balances his or her life and faith is up to them. Spiritual directors will give guidance, and they have all the resources of Opus Dei to turn to, but the prelature does not dictate how they should make decisions at work, politically or concerning their general lifestyle. For many Opus Dei members, it is easier to say nothing to

NUMERARIES

FOR EVERY NUMERARY, THE FIRST TASK UPON WAKING IS TO KISS THE FLOOR AND SAY, IN PRAYER, THE LATIN WORD "SERVIAM" WHICH MEANS "I WILL SERVE". THE DAY BEGINS WITH MASS IN THE CHAPEL AT THE CENTRE WHERE THE NUMERARY LIVES (WHICH IS KNOWN AS AN ORATORY) AND, IDEALLY, THE REST OF THE PRAYERS AND SPIRITUAL PRACTICES KNOWN WITHIN OPUS DEI AS THE "NORMS" ARE CARRIED OUT AT REGULAR INTERVALS THROUGHOUT THE DAY.

RIGHT Sam Pleasants, numerary and director of Ashwell House, the Opus Dei-run hostel for women in Islington, London, pictured with some of the student residents. Young women from all over the world reside here while at college or university.

BELOW The life of a numerary is spiritually challenging, and requires maintaining a balance between an insular life in a centre, with its rituals of prayer, and having a normal job in the everyday world. Escrivá's vision was for numeraries to be without the cares of family ties, so that they could focus their efforts on bringing Christianity into the outside world.

Numeraries with outside jobs have to find time in the working day for seclusion and prayer. Those who work in Opus Dei centres or hostels may choose to pray together or alone. In addition, numeraries are expected to attend meetings, circles, retreats, meditation and workshop sessions and to provide spiritual direction for other members of Opus Dei. For those numeraries who work in Opus Dei hostels, the day continues into the evening with supervision, talks, events and discussions with the students, and many of them take very little time off.

COMMITMENT

For the first 18 months of being a numerary, each person is on probation; after that, for five years, he or she has an annually renewable contract with

Opus Dei. Every 19 March, numeraries can either renew this contract or not. If it is not renewed, the person automatically leaves the prelature. After six and a half years, the numerary can make the "Fidelity" or commitment for life, after which some choose to wear a ring on their wedding finger. Once the Fidelity is made, a numerary does not have to renew it and, if they wish to leave, they are required to write a letter to ask for dispensation. If they do not make the Fidelity, they must either leave or change their vocation to become a supernumerary.

CELIBACY AND SEGREGATION

Numeraries live a celibate life in an Opus Dei centre. Men and women live separately and have little contact with each other. Where both sexes have centres in the same building, they have separate entrances. This works all the way down the line: there is one governing body for the women and

another for the men, both based in Rome. As avowed celibates, they must not only keep their promise but also be seen to be keeping it. Thus, any necessary communication is made by e-mail, letter or telephone wherever possible.

Opus Dei's policy is based on the view that men and woman are different and respond in different ways to spiritual direction. Therefore, segregation should mean that each sex will be better served spiritually. A priest giving a talk to the women will address them in different terms from those he would use with men, using different examples. Also, spiritual directors within Opus Dei give "formation" and counselling to their own sex as they are more likely to understand the struggles that may be taking place. Female numeraries, however, take Mass and receive confession from a priest, and male numeraries are cooked for and looked after by female assistant numeraries. Women numeraries may wear fashionable clothes, colour their hair and wear make-up and jewellery if they wish, however, they are not permitted to smoke, whereas the men can.

ABOVE A Mass at the men's chapel at the Opus Dei headquarters in New York. The Mass is the most important part of the day to any Catholic, and the observants are expected to attend Mass every day. Participants are united with Christ through the taking of his blood and body through the communion wine and bread.

SCREENING MAIL
One of the scandals that has surrounded Opus Dei is the accusation that mail sent to numeraries is opened and read by centre directors. The screening of mail was once a common practice in religious orders as well as in boarding schools and other Catholic institutions. It was intended to be a way of ensuring that there were no hidden troubles or challenges in the recipient's life, but it is acknowledged throughout the Church that it has been open to abuse. The majority of Catholic organizations have abandoned the practice, and Opus Dei say that it is no longer done within their portals despite claims by ex-numeraries that, in some centres, it is still done. With the advent of e-mail, the screening of mail would be virtually impossible to maintain.

LEFT St Francis of Assisi receiving confession. Confession is the way that Catholics admit to making errors. Each person must confess their sins and be given penance and absolution by the priest before attending Mass. Once a sin is absolved, it no longer exists. It is thought to be vital for a Catholic to make a final confession before dying.

In a world where workplaces have communal washrooms and gentlemen's clubs have been abolished, this is an old-fashioned and politically incorrect reality, but members of Opus Dei are in the organization of their own volition and either accept how they live or choose to leave.

NUMERARY ASSISTANTS

OPUS DEI HAS ABOUT 4,000 NUMERARY ASSISTANTS WORLDWIDE WHO, TOGETHER WITH SOME NUMERARIES, WORK FULL-TIME TAKING CARE OF OPUS DEI CENTRES, HOSTELS AND EDUCATIONAL FACILITIES. THE IDEA FOR CELIBATE WOMEN HOUSEKEEPERS CAME FROM ESCRIVÁ'S OWN FAMILY LIFE, IN WHICH HIS MOTHER AND SISTER TOOK CARE OF THE FIRST MEMBERS. HE WANTED OPUS DEI CENTRES TO FEEL LIKE HOMES, SO NUMERARY ASSISTANTS FUNCTION AS THE MOTHERS OF OPUS DEI. THIS WAS ESCRIVÁ'S VISION, AND OPUS DEI DOES NOT BELIEVE IT SHOULD CHANGE.

RIGHT Finding joy in everyday repetitive tasks is one of the greatest challenges for the spiritual seeker. Assistant numeraries in Opus Dei are considered to be spiritual carers and are greatly valued for their work.

BELOW Staff preparing meals at the Opus Dei-run Ashwell House hostel for girls in north London.

Members of Opus Dei believe that women have an aptitude for home-making that men lack. British numerary Eileen Cole was quoted in the *Scotsman* newspaper as saying: "If we didn't do it, they would be living like savages. Women are simply better at these things than men."

Escrivá called the work that numerary assistants do the "apostolate of apostolates" because it is they who give the centres the family atmosphere that characterizes Opus Dei. While the modern world sees this as demeaning to women, it is clear that the women working as numerary assistants do not agree. Although they are called "assistants" their work is a vocation demanding a full-time

commitment and the willingness to live without a husband or children. Like numeraries, their lives include spiritual formation and self-mortification.

Assistant numeraries are like all other people working in the service industries, therefore some are qualified and some are not. Younger people in catering work have National Vocational Qualifications in the UK, Europe and the USA, and equivalent qualifications in other countries. Many assistant numeraries hold NVQs and other nationally recognized qualifications such as Health & Safety, Food Hygiene, WSET diplomas in Wines and Spirits and Key Skills. There are many ways of qualifying, either through attending full-time courses at colleges or training centres or alternatively on a day release basis or on-the-job through a training provider. Some of the assistant numeraries have also become qualified as NVQ assessors to facilitate in-house training. An assistant numerary's work is regarded

LEFT A nun mopping the floor in a church in Venice, Italy. In all religious orders, a regular routine of carrying out housework, gardening, cooking and other basic practical tasks is considered essential for the understanding of humility and the value of the mundane. It would be considered spiritual arrogance to regard such work as demeaning.

BIBLE EXAMPLES

Jesus Christ set the example of willing service to others when he washed his disciples' feet in the Gospel of John. He insisted on doing so despite Simon Peter's resistance, saying: "You also ought to wash one another's feet. For I have given you an example, that you should do as I have done to you" (John 10:14-17.) Another Biblical example is the woman with the Alabaster box in Luke 7:44 who washed Jesus' feet. Later, the same woman, identified as Mary of Bethany in John 11:2, is invited to sit at Jesus' feet and learn from him while her sister, Martha, grumbles about having to cook (Luke 10:39).

as being different from that of a cook, bar person, waitress or house-keeper in a hotel; the main difference is their spiritual commitment. Assistant numeraries often hire other women to help them with cleaning and everyday jobs.

A TYPICAL DAY

In London's Ashwell House hostel for girls, the numerary assistants' day starts with prayer and Mass just like the numeraries'. They then prepare breakfast for the 40 or so young women who live in the hostel and for the numeraries who run it. The kitchen at Ashwell House is fitted out like a modern restaurant kitchen and is kept spotlessly clean. Once the girls have left for college, the assistants spend the day in prayer, shopping, washing clothes and bed linen, preparing for supper and cleaning. Their prayer life is identical to that of numeraries. Supper is served at 7.30 p.m., and after washing up, they will often have evening activities with their friends at the centre.

COMPARISON WITH NUNS

Both monks and nuns have always been expected to carry out work including cleaning, gardening, cooking, sewing and washing. In a religious life such work is seen as an important part of spiritual development. If such tasks were viewed as demeaning or menial, it would mean that the monk or nun had not understood the nature of spirituality and Christian service. To serve others is a true sanctification of work.

Numerary assistants generally wear uniforms, which are similar to those worn by secular hotel staff. Like all numeraries of Opus Dei, numerary assistants have the choice of whether they stay or leave on an annual basis. They, too, can make the lifetime's commitment known as the Fidelity but, again, are free to leave if they decide to do so. Unlike a monk or nun who might choose to leave a monastery, many of them have a qualification which would help them find work elsewhere if they were to leave.

BELOW Christ washing his disciples' feet, from the back panels of La Maesta (Majesty), painted in 1308 for the high altar of Siena Cathedral, Italy.

ASSOCIATES AND CO-OPERATORS

BOTH ASSOCIATES AND CO-OPERATORS OF OPUS DEI LIVE IN THEIR OWN HOMES; THE MAJOR DIFFERENCE BETWEEN THE TWO IS THAT ASSOCIATES ARE COMMITTED, CELIBATE, FULL MEMBERS OF OPUS DEI JUST LIKE NUMERARIES, WHILE CO-OPERATORS ARE THE EQUIVALENT OF FRIENDS OF THE FAMILY. TO BE A CO-OPERATOR YOU DO NOT EVEN HAVE TO BE A CHRISTIAN, ALTHOUGH THE MAJORITY OF CO-OPERATORS WITHIN OPUS DEI ARE FELLOW CATHOLICS.

RIGHT Opus Dei is unusual in the Catholic Church in that it allows its members different levels of commitment according to their personal and family situation. However, at whatever level people decide to join, every member is expected to live as an evangelical Catholic.

BELOW Arnold Hall Conference Centre, in Boston, USA. Hundreds of people attend for weekend retreats, Catholic doctrine studies and professional ethics seminars each year.

ASSOCIATES

People may become associates if they are unable to study or serve with Opus Dei in the same way as numeraries, because of a particular personal situation that requires them to remain living at home or elsewhere.

Associates live similar lives to numeraries, except that they only rarely live in an Opus Dei centre. This includes living a celibate lifestyle, carrying out the "norms" and attending circles, seminars and retreats. Being an associate is a role most suitable for those whose job requires them to live on site, to give more than usual levels of commitment, or for someone who has a family who needs them to be at home. In many ways it is one of the hardest ways to be an Opus Dei

member, as there is none of the immediate support and companionship that numeraries living in the Opus Dei centres have. On the other hand, the associate has more freedom to live as he or she wishes, as there is no direct daily supervision.

CO-OPERATORS

The work of a co-operator is at the opposite end of the scale to that of an assistant and is the least demanding way to be involved with Opus Dei. Co-operators are friends of Opus Dei rather than members, although they attend regular meetings and believe in Opus Dei principles. Opus Dei has approximately 164,000 co-operators worldwide, most of whom are women. As well as individuals, religious communities can also become co-operators of Opus Dei. Their contribution consists of daily prayer for the evangelizing work of the prelature. At present, more than 500 communities of both men and women support the prelature with their prayers in many countries throughout the world.

INTER-FAITH CO-OPERATORS

Opus Dei has co-operators who are Jews, Muslims and Buddhists as well as Christians of other denominations. In fact, Opus Dei was the first Catholic organization that was given approval by the Vatican, in 1950, to enrol non-Catholics. What all co-operators share is a common desire to participate and collaborate in various initiatives of the prelature. While in theory Opus Dei members, together with all Catholics, believe that the only path to God is through Jesus Christ, the modern world accepts and promotes inter-faith movements. More and more, Opus Dei is opening up to people of all faiths who have a similar vision of spiritual inspiration, formation and sanctification.

Outsiders may suspect that this is an attempt to evangelize and draw in more members, which may well be true, as Opus Dei's foundational principle is to promote both Catholicism and its own beliefs in the world. It is no different in Opus Dei than in any other proselytizing faith. At Ashwell House, the women's hostel in London, more girls originally from other faiths become baptized Catholics than existing Catholics join Opus Dei.

LEVELS OF COMMITMENT

Co-operators are offered similar activities to members of Opus Dei and are free to attend weekly classes, meditations and retreats. Whereas an associate is expected to be committed to The Work and give all the time and spare money that is available to him or her, co-operators may attend when they want to do so, give what donations they wish instead of being expected to give regular amounts, and may even be active members of another religion entirely. For many co-operators who are Catholics, or Christians of other denominations, involvement with Opus Dei has helped them to become closer to their own church and taught them to live the principles of sanctifying work and everyday life. Opus Dei co-operators also include Catholic priests, monks and nuns who are devoted to their own diocese or religious order but who still value the sense of spiritual devotion and community that comes with being a part of Opus Dei. The issue of members being obliged to give money to Opus Dei does not arise in the case of those living a religious life, who have no possessions or money of their own.

ABOVE Any or all of these people could be members of Opus Dei. They each have different jobs, homes, educational backgrounds, languages and nationalities. The common aspiration and benchmark for all Opus Dei members is a high standard of morality, as they perceive it, in everyday life.

LEFT Anne Jose Varavukala of New Delhi, India, moved to the USA with her family to undertake studies in specialized education and look after her autistic son. "Opus Dei has given me a great comfort in learning how many graces we receive in the sacraments of confession and Holy Communion. All this has helped me accept my son's handicap with gladness, seeing it as a gift from God."

JOINING OPUS DEI

NOWADAYS, OPUS DEI HAS FIRM RULES FOR PEOPLE WISHING TO JOIN. AS WITH MOST GROUPS THAT HAVE GROWN ORGANICALLY OVER DECADES, THIS HAS NOT ALWAYS BEEN THE CASE. FROM THE OBSERVATIONS OF CRITICAL EX-MEMBERS, IT APPEARS THAT NOT ALL THOSE WHO HAVE JOINED OVER THE YEARS REALIZED EXACTLY HOW MUCH OF A COMMITMENT THEY WERE MAKING, NOR WHAT THEIR LIFESTYLE WOULD BE. HOWEVER, WITH SO MUCH PUBLICITY ABOUT OPUS DEI AVAILABLE ON THE INTERNET AND SO MUCH CONTROVERSY ARISING FROM THE BOOK *THE DA VINCI CODE*, THE PRELATURE HAS BECOME MUCH MORE PUBLIC, INCLUDING POSTING SECTIONS ABOUT JOINING OPUS DEI ON ITS WEBSITE.

RIGHT Two teenage girls at a Harambee 2002 convention. Opus Dei has received criticism for its recruitment methods, especially with young people who may lack the maturity to resist pressure. Matthew Collins, an ex-member with no axe to grind, states on his Internet blogsite: "While I can't say that no one in Opus Dei has ever put undue pressure on a young person to join, I can say that it absolutely did not happen in my case and it does not happen in most cases."

What is clear – and should always have been clear – is that becoming a member of Opus Dei is a vocation, a "calling from God". Escrivá coined the word "whistling" for people wanting to join Opus Dei. He compared the process with a kettle beginning to boil after heating up for a long time. An applicant is expected to get permission from the Opus Dei centre that he or she is attending before "whistling". This involves writing a letter of application and, if permission is granted, the applicant requests admission in writing. Admission is granted after a minimum of six months from the date of the letter of application. Someone as young as 16 years old may "whistle", although they must be 18 before being accepted into Opus Dei.

COMMITMENT

Members of Opus Dei commit to a contract called the "Oblation". In return for Opus Dei agreeing to provide doctrinal and spiritual formation, they agree to live in the spirit of The Work. For the first five years, this contract must be renewed annually on 19 March, in order to continue with membership of Opus Dei. The date is significant as being the feast of St Joseph, earthly father of Jesus, who was made patron saint of the Universal Church by Pope Pius IX in 1847. A minimum of five years after making the first contractual declaration (which would be six and a half years after making the first application), the member may make his or her "Fidelity", which is

RIGHT An English family praying at the tomb of St Josemaría in Rome. Opus Dei members all share a strong sense of vocation – a lifelong commitment to God. This can be inexplicable to anyone who has not felt the calling to a life of service. Many people who feel the calling to faith face strong opposition from friends and family who find it incomprehensible.

a lifetime commitment, although not a vow such as would be made by a monk or nun. Should a numerary or associate choose not to make the Fidelity, then they would have to leave. If, however, they chose to change their vocation to become a supernumerary before the Oblation, they would be allowed to do so. Supernumeraries may also make the Fidelity, but it can be after five years or much later – or not at all, if they wish.

RECRUITMENT POLICY

One of the criticisms of Opus Dei has been over its over-zealous recruitment policy. The Internet is littered with comments and articles by people who declined to join but felt that they were being railroaded into making a decision by Opus Dei members. In *Conversations with Monsignor Escrivá*, Escrivá is quoted as saying: "The decisions that determine the course of an entire life ... should be taken calmly, without rushing into it. Such decisions should be particularly responsible and prudent. And part of prudence consists precisely in seeking advice ... of other people, and especially of one's parents." However, in 1968, in Opus Dei's magazine, *Crónica*, he wrote: "None of my children can rest satisfied if he doesn't win four or five faithful vocations each year", and in other editions of the journal he wrote, "We do not have any other aim than the corporate one: proselytism, winning vocations." Given those differing comments, individual Opus Dei members would be likely to have very diverse views on how much pressure is appropriate when a possible new member expresses enthusiasm about The Work.

FAMILIES SIDELINED

Young people can make a tentative approach to become a member of Opus Dei at sixteen-and-a-half years old, and this is one of the practices that worry critics. However, most of those who express an interest in joining are young people who are already involved in Opus Dei through the activities of parents and other relatives. Opus Dei representatives say that, on average, fewer than one per cent of the young people living in hostels express an interest in joining Opus Dei. A slightly larger percentage become attracted to Catholicism and will join the Church but prefer a less taxing lifestyle than that of a member of Opus Dei.

Many families have complained that their children or relatives did not consult them about joining Opus Dei and that they were "frozen out" of the applicant's life after they did join. There is a long tradition in the Catholic faith of aspirants to ordination or the holy life turning their backs on their families. Saints, especially, are renowned for leaving home and family to follow their vocation. Those with a genuine vocation will not bow to opposition. Those without one cannot possibly see any sense or logic in the decisions being made. There is no doubt that vocations to join Opus Dei have left many relatives shocked, upset and confused.

ABOVE Brafa, an Opus Dei-run school in Nou Barri, a working-class district of Barcelona, Spain, was founded in 1953. It runs sporting competitions for people of all ages as well as offering courses of Christian education.

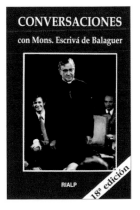

ABOVE *Conversations with Monsignor Escrivá*, which contains seven press interviews that Josemaría gave between 1966 and 1968.

LEFT Once a potential applicant has been recommended by an Opus Dei centre, they must write a letter of application and wait a full six months before being accepted.

LEAVING OPUS DEI

TECHNICALLY, ANYONE CAN LEAVE OPUS DEI AT ANY TIME EITHER BY WALKING OUT OF THE DOOR OR BY NOT SHOWING UP TO ANY MORE SERVICES OR MEETINGS. HOWEVER, THE REALITY IS OFTEN MORE COMPLEX. ALL MEMBERS OF OPUS DEI SHOULD HAVE A VOCATION — A DEEP, INNER, SPIRITUAL COMMITMENT TO WHAT THEY ARE DOING. SHOULD THAT FAIL, IT CAN BE A VERY UPSETTING TIME BOTH FOR THE PERSON CONCERNED AND FOR THEIR FRIENDS AND COLLEAGUES IN OPUS DEI. THERE ARE NO FIGURES AVAILABLE TO INDICATE WHAT PERCENTAGE OF MEMBERS LEAVE THE PRELATURE, BUT IT HAS BEEN ESTIMATED AT ABOUT 25 PER CENT.

RIGHT Leaving Opus Dei has been a lonely and frightening experience for many people who felt they were being pressured to stay.

BELOW Catholic hardliners Pope John Paul II, Cardinal Ratzinger and Venezuelan Archbishop Rosalio José Lara (right) signing the Code of Canon Law in 1983. The code was seen as a signal of support for staunchly Catholic groups, such as Opus Dei, who promote allegiance to the Church's viewpoint on issues such as marriage and abortion.

There are several different ways to leave Opus Dei. Before making the Fidelity, members have to renew their membership every year; if they do not do so, then they are no longer a part of Opus Dei. After the Fidelity, they are expected to write a letter requesting to leave but, in fact, those who wish to leave often just walk away.

In theory, spiritual directors and priests should be well aware of any Opus Dei member's wavering vocation; it is their duty to be observant and supportive of the person's faith and spiritual direction. Likewise, the person having doubts would be considered to be in error if they

concealed those doubts from their advisors and, given the regular groups, circles, retreats and meditations within Opus Dei, it would be quite difficult for them to do so.

PRESSURE TO REMAIN

To members of Opus Dei, it is a grave matter for someone to turn away from The Work once they have completed their first 18 months within the prelature. For an ultra-orthodox Catholic, abandoning a vocation would be considered a genuinely dreadful thing to do. A vocation is intended to be for life, as is marriage. Orthodox Catholics would have no sympathy with a husband or wife who walked out on a marriage, believing that, whatever the issue, it could be

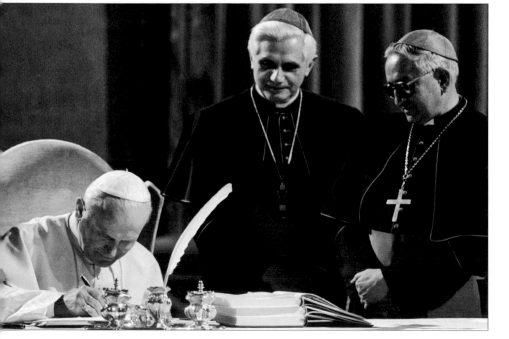

PUTTING YOUR SOUL IN PERIL

Today many Opus Dei members, particularly in Western Europe, are more comfortable with the idea of people finding their own path to God. However, those with ultra-orthodox Catholic views believe that turning away from a vocation would mean putting the soul in danger of damnation. According to dozens of testimonies posted on the Internet, particularly to the Opus Dei Awareness Network (ODAN), this has been said to people who wanted to leave or who had left, causing considerable emotional distress and anger. Tammy DiNicola, co-founder of ODAN, claims that new members are typically told that if they leave Opus Dei they may be damned and will absolutely live their whole life without God's grace.

resolved through prayer, confession and counselling, and that the commitment was all-important. For these reasons, many people who have left Opus Dei have reported intense pressure from their colleagues to remain.

While accepting that many members of Opus Dei are very happy, former numerary Dr John Roche is still highly critical of the prelature's attitude to those who want to leave. On the Opus Dei Awareness Network (ODAN) website, he wrote: "Members who criticize and think of leaving ... are told, untruthfully, that those who leave bitterly regret it, are called traitors, and if they persist are expelled without a penny. As a result there are a lot of very disturbed people in Opus Dei living a kind of horror without escape, which only a religious conscience can experience. I know of several cases of virtual house arrest and interrogation and of attempted and perhaps even successful suicides." Dr Roche adds: "Those who do leave are sometimes subjected to systematic defamation, which also explains why many former members are afraid to speak out." Opus Dei denies these claims, but Dr Roche, in 2006, confirmed for this book that he stood by his views.

ABOVE Catholics believe that turning away from the Church means turning away from God and being condemned to hell. Opus Dei members who believe this have been known to put pressure on people to stay in order to try and save their souls.

LEFT Tammy DiNicola, a former member of Opus Dei, with her mother Dianne, browsing a list of forbidden literature, banned by Opus Dei. They run ODAN, which provides information about Opus Dei and support to people who have been adversely affected by it.

PART FOUR

OPUS DEI IN THE CORPORATE WORLD

 Escrivá described Opus Dei as "a disorganized organization", and it can be a challenge for the outsider to understand the fine line of where the prelature begins and ends in the business world. For Opus Dei, a "corporate work" is a project that is run by Opus Dei members together with others outside the prelature. Opus Dei provides spiritual background and guidance, appoints chaplains and religious instructors, and will oversee the board to ensure that the institution is being run according to the essence of The Work. Opus Dei does not own the assets of its corporate works, but as all its members give financial support to the prelature, it will benefit from their financial successes.

RIGHT The regional headquarters of Opus Dei in the USA are in Manhattan, in New York City. The impressive building is a $47 million, 12,300 square metre (133,000 square foot) purpose-built centre on Lexington Avenue.

CORPORATE WORKS

OPUS DEI CORPORATE WORKS ARE ALL WITHIN THE SPHERES OF EDUCATION, SOCIAL SERVICES AND HEALTH. THEY INCLUDE SCHOOLS, UNIVERSITIES, VOCATIONAL TRAINING CENTRES, AGRICULTURAL SCHOOLS AND COLLEGES, STUDENT HOSTELS, MEDICAL CLINICS, AND SCHOOLS OF DOMESTIC SCIENCE. IN ADDITION, OPUS DEI MEMBERS WILL OFTEN GROUP TOGETHER TO START A PROJECT THAT THEY RUN ACCORDING TO OPUS DEI PRINCIPLES BUT THAT IS *NOT* A CORPORATE WORK. THE PROJECT MAY CONTINUE TO BE INDEPENDENT, OR IT MAY APPLY TO BECOME A CORPORATE WORK WITH OPUS DEI MEMBERS SERVING ON THE BOARD OF DIRECTORS.

RIGHT Monkole, in Kinshasa, in the Democratic Republic of the Congo, is an Opus Dei-funded hospital that attends to thousands of people in situations of extreme need. Attached to Monkole is the Higher Institute of Nursing, which prepares young women for the nursing profession.

BELOW The University of Navarra campus in Pamplona, Spain, where emphasis is placed on personal education: there is a ratio of one teacher to six students (2,421 lecturers for 12,025 undergraduates).

Many of the fears around Opus Dei as a "secret" organization stem from the fact that individual members work in hundreds of companies and associations around the world that are, no doubt, influenced in some way by their beliefs. Inside Opus Dei, the doctrinal and spiritual teaching focuses exclusively on the doctrine of Catholic faith and, therefore, wherever there is an Opus Dei member, there is an active representative of Catholic teaching and ethics. However, outside of that, every member will make whatever business decisions their particular strengths and experience guide them towards. There is no Opus Dei stance on how business should be transacted.

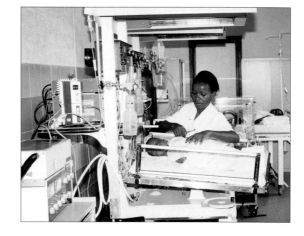

ELITISM

Opus Dei is often accused of being elitist because much of its observable work in the Western world is in the field of education in the private sector. Its most easily identifiable corporate work is fairly high profile, such as the Heights School in Potomac, Maryland, USA, the Institute for Higher Business Studies (IESE) in Barcelona and the University of Navarra, both in Spain, or the University of Strathmore in Nairobi, Kenya. Some members of the prelature also run their own high-profile initiatives, which are *not* Opus Dei corporate works. One such venture is the Rome Reports television news agency, which was launched by an Opus Dei numerary to focus on Catholic news. Members of Opus Dei run numerous foundations promoting education and social welfare in the developing world, many carrying charitable status.

CHARITY WORK

One of the best-known charities run by Opus Dei is Harambee 2002, a venture in Africa with the aim of "thanking God for the canonization of Escrivá" by offering practical social projects. Smaller charitable efforts include a group of Irish, Finnish, American, Lithuanian and Latvian students spending two weeks a year in St Petersburg as part of a service project with the Dom Miloserdia Centre, a charity agency of the Russian Orthodox Church. The young men renovate and re-decorate five apartments in the centre of the city for Russian families identified by the charity agency in the city. In Spain, the Sansueña School of Zaragoza organizes a "Day of Solidarity", a campaign in which students promote various fund-raising initiatives for social projects. In recent years, funds have been collected for women's centres in India, Poland and Lithuania; for welfare projects in Bolivia and Nigeria; and for aid to needy families in Zaragoza.

FINANCING THE WORK

Money and Christianity have always been controversial subjects, partly due to the wealth of certain parts of the Catholic and Anglican churches. A common belief is that people who follow Christ should be poor and humble and that they should expect their reward in heaven. Religious organizations are often wealthy because their followers are encouraged to give them money. Members of Opus Dei are expected to give all that they can reasonably afford to the organization, both to help it with daily expenses and in spreading its evangelical mission to the world.

RULES OF DONATION

There is no specific amount that any Opus Dei member should give. Numeraries, associates and friendly ex-members say that enough money should be kept for the everyday needs of oneself and one's family, and the remainder given to Opus Dei as it

is their responsibility to support the needs and services of the prelature. Some ex-members say that numeraries are required to give too much, but current numeraries say that no examination is made of their earnings, and how much they give is up to them. Numeraries have their own individual bank accounts and autonomy over their own finances. Although they are not members of religious orders and do not take formal vows of poverty, chastity and obedience, numeraries attempt to live a life of modesty in financial as well as spiritual matters. Supernumeraries and associates are not expected to give as much as numeraries, as they have family commitments.

HOW WEALTHY IS OPUS DEI?

The financial value of all of Opus Dei's corporate works is £1.5 billion (US$2.8 billion), just slightly more than the Archdiocese of Chicago, in the USA, which has reported assets of £1.4 billion. However, Opus Dei has 85,000 members worldwide and the Archdiocese has a Catholic population of 2.3 million people, so it is clear that the donations and support per capita within Opus Dei are much higher. Opus Dei is not a business corporation, nor is it a limited company. As it is funded by contributions from its supporters, some areas are far wealthier than others. In the UK, donations go to the Opus Dei Charitable Trust.

ABOVE Harambee 2002 sponsors educational projects in and about Africa. In the Swahili dialect, Harambee means "all for one" or "working together". It is the cry of fishermen as they drag their nets ashore and is meant to resound with collective efforts made for the common good, such as helping a family in need or building a new school or church.

BELOW American churches are often extremely wealthy through the tithes of their members, who are taught to put God first financially.

OPUS DEI AND EDUCATION

OPUS DEI'S CORPORATE WORK IN THE EDUCATION SECTOR ENCOMPASSES 15 UNIVERSITIES, 11 BUSINESS SCHOOLS, 36 PRIMARY AND SECONDARY SCHOOLS, 97 TECHNICAL SCHOOLS AND 166 UNIVERSITY RESIDENCES THROUGHOUT THE WORLD. THERE ARE OTHER ORGANIZATIONS TOO, THAT OPUS DEI DOES NOT REGARD AS CORPORATE WORKS BUT FOR WHICH IT DOES PROVIDE SPIRITUAL ADVICE. THESE INCLUDE TWO UNIVERSITIES, A BUSINESS SCHOOL, 213 PRIMARY AND SECONDARY SCHOOLS AND 59 VOCATIONAL SCHOOLS.

RIGHT Students at La Pedreira, a technical school for men and boys, in one of the poorest neighbourhoods of São Paulo in Brazil.

BELOW Bishop Javier Echevarría being shown around an Opus Dei-run school in Santiago, Chile. The prelature is hugely popular in South America, one of the most strongly Catholic parts the world. Religious education is seen as vital there both for economic development and to promote an end to corruption.

A school run by members of Opus Dei is not considered "an Opus Dei school", and it will not be called "Opus Dei Junior School" or "St Josemaría High School". However, the formation within the school will be that of Opus Dei, many of the children will be those of supernumeraries, and it will be clear that it is a Catholic school working within Christian principles.

Opus Dei secondary schools are not only single-sex, but the faculties are segregated as well, so that men teach at a boys' school and women at a girls' school. The majority of schools run by Opus Dei members are in developing countries where education is desperately needed and societies are less concerned about equal opportunities for boys and girls.

UNIVERSITIES

Opus Dei has 15 corporate work universities and business schools, none of which are single-sex. The first, the University of Navarra, was founded by Escrivá in Pamplona, Spain, in 1952. It has 20 faculties and institutes, including a university hospital and a business school, the Institute for Higher Business Studies (IESE), which is located in Barcelona. The others include universities in Rome; Chicago, USA; Nairobi; Lima; Santiago; and Pasig City in the Philippines. All the universities emphasize spirituality at work. Although they are open to men and women, the hostels associated with them are single-sex, with strict rules about visits from the opposite sex.

YOUNG PEOPLE'S CLUBS AND SOCIETIES

Opus Dei has hundreds of youth clubs and groups for young people worldwide. These are individually organized by supernumeraries, numeraries,

In the more secular Western world, with street-wise attitudes widespread, some potential recipients are suspicious about the underlying religious motives of such schemes, and Opus Dei's detractors are concerned about what the Opus Dei Awareness Network calls "undue influence" over the young. However, Opus Dei is at pains to emphasize that projects such as *Reach Out!* encourage student tutors of any religion and also those with none. Often the need for practical help and positive role models for young people, whether in disadvantaged inner-city areas in the West, or in poor communities in developing countries, is so great that the projects are widely welcomed.

associates and co-operators and are open to young people of all races and religions. They are often based around sporting activities and are run as both unisex and single-sex groups. Spiritual formation is available through all those that are run by Opus Dei members, with access to further information, pilgrimages, retreats, talks and groups. Just how obvious the Opus Dei influence is varies according to the location and organizers. At the hostels run by Opus Dei members there are meditations, church services and discussions and each room contains a crucifix or religious picture.

In Manchester, UK, Opus Dei sponsors *Reach Out!*, an Inner City Youth Achievement Programme in which university students and professionals work with young people in disadvantaged parts of the city, helping them with their school studies. Currently, *Reach Out!* works with boys aged eight to 14, but there is a separate, parallel programme in which a group of women students organize activities for girls and young females. It aims to help as many young people as possible reach college in an area where university entrance is uncommon.

Reach Out! includes an intensive summer programme in which children, led by the students, dedicate two to three weeks of their summer holidays to mathematics, English and science, mixed with sports, crafts and other activities.

LEFT The University of La Sabana in Bogotá, Colombia, one of many Opus Dei educational initiatives at tertiary level. The Sabana Mission, formed of volunteers from the university, provides help to families in the neighbourhoods of Bojacá, Fonquetá, Mercedes de Calahorra and Las Delicias, all part of the township of Chía, a community close to the university.

ABOVE Basic education in one of the poorest communities in Santiago, Chile. Nocedal Technical School provides basic and intermediate education to 500 children and teenagers. The school offers technical courses to train pupils in electronics and telecommunications.

LEFT An Opus Dei volunteer helping out on the *Reach Out!* youth achievement programme in Manchester, UK.

KEY OPUS DEI CHURCHES

THERE ARE MORE THAN A DOZEN CHURCHES IN THE CARE OF OPUS DEI PRIESTS WORLDWIDE, INCLUDING CHURCHES IN SPAIN, GERMANY, HOLLAND, AUSTRIA, ITALY, THE UK AND THE USA. EVERY OPUS DEI CENTRE HAS ITS OWN ORATORY, BUT THESE ARE NOT OPEN TO THE GENERAL PUBLIC. ROME HAS THREE OPUS DEI CHURCHES: THE FIRST CHURCH GIVEN TO OPUS DEI FOR MINISTRY IN THE 1960S WAS ST GIOVANNI BATTISTA (ST JOHN THE BAPTIST), IN COLLATINO, ROME. ST EUGENIO IN THE PARIOLI DISTRICT OF ROME WAS ENTRUSTED TO OPUS DEI IN THE 1980S, AND THE THIRD ROMAN CHURCH, ST APOLLINARE, IS A CHAPEL WITHIN THE OPUS DEI-RUN UNIVERSITY OF SANTA CROCE.

In the USA, there is only one full Opus Dei church – Our Lady of the Angels, in Chicago. However, in Washington DC, the Catholic Information Office is run by an Opus Dei priest and has a chapel inside, where daily Mass is celebrated. Our Lady of the Angels Church was opened in 1920 as the Polish Basilica, in Chicago, but was closed and marked for demolition in 1988 due to unsafe conditions. At the request of Cardinal Bernardin, then Archbishop of Chicago, Opus Dei assumed responsibility for the parish in 1991, and the church restoration started later that year, including major repairs of the dome, the

BELOW The church of Our Lady of the Angels, in Chicago, finished primarily by Polish immigrants in 1920.

roofs, the stained-glass windows and 26 roof angels, which needed to be fully rebuilt. The church is open daily and celebrates Sunday Masses in English, Polish and Spanish. It has its own school for boys and another for girls.

Opus Dei's theological influence is made evident by Santa Croce in Italy – the Pontifical University of the Holy Cross – which is a centre for university-level studies in ecclesiastical sciences. It is made up of four Schools: Theology, Canon Law, Philosophy and Social Institutional Communication, all of which have full canonical power to confer Bachelor, Licentiate and Doctoral degrees.

The Higher Institute of Religious Sciences at Apollinare is academically connected with the School of Theology. It uses a special method of learning by correspondence and is a place of training for Opus Dei priests. The chapel of St Apollinare itself is known for its concerts, especially Gregorian chanting.

THE CHURCH IN THE UK

In January 2005, Cardinal Cormac Murphy-O'Connor, Archbishop of Westminster, gave pastoral care of St Thomas More Church, Swiss Cottage, London, to Father Gerard Sheehan, an Opus Dei priest. Father Sheehan was deanery secretary in the diocese before his appointment, as well as working at Netherhall House, the

ABOVE A statue of Opus Dei founder Josemaría Escrivá in an exterior niche of St Peter's Basilica, Rome.

student residence run by Opus Dei nearby. Opus Dei itself has had a presence in the parish of St Thomas More for more than 50 years.

When announcing the appointment, Cardinal Murphy-O'Connor said, in a statement: "The members of Opus Dei have their own particular part to play in the mission of the Church in our country. Father Sheehan's appointment is a further sign of that commitment and a natural development of his longstanding engagement in the parish." The Cardinal added that the appointment continued the Diocese of Wesminster's policy of entrusting some parishes to communities and movements that were making a significant contribution to the Church's life. Before the appointment of Father Sheehan, Westminster had already entrusted two parishes to Vietnamese and Brazilian communities living in London. The diocese is also looking at ways in which other ecclesiastic groups, including the Neo-Catechumenate and the Carmelites of Mary Immaculate, may be able to take on further pastoral duties in the diocese. In each case, the priests concerned come under the direct jurisdiction of the diocese, responsible to the Cardinal.

RESERVATION AND RECOMMENDATION

The previous Archbishop of Westminster and spiritual leader of the Catholic Church in England from 1976 to 1999, Cardinal Basil Hume, had serious reservations about Opus Dei, particularly its recruitment techniques. His advisor in such matters was Father Vladimir Felzmann, a former numerary and chaplain at Netherhall House in London, and a strong critic of some of Opus Dei's practices. In 1981, Cardinal Hume published a set of "recommendations" for Opus Dei in his archdiocese. These were that no one below the age of 18 should be allowed to make any long-term commitment to the prelature; that young people who wanted to join should discuss the matter with their parents or guardians; and that people should be free to join or leave the organization without "undue pressure". He also said that the activities of Opus Dei in Westminster should be clearly identifiable.

However, Cardinal Hume was not totally opposed to the prelature. He said a Mass for Opus Dei members in 1998, when they were celebrating the 70th anniversary of Escrivá's vision.

OPUS DEI IN AFRICA

THERE ARE MORE THAN ONE MILLION CATHOLICS IN AFRICA. IN 1958, OPUS DEI BEGAN WORK IN KENYA, FOLLOWED BY NIGERIA IN 1965, CONGO AND THE IVORY COAST IN 1980, CAMEROON IN 1988, UGANDA IN 1996 AND SOUTH AFRICA IN 1998. IT HAS ALSO CONTRIBUTED FINANCIALLY TO PROJECTS IN SUDAN AND MADAGASCAR, WHERE IT DOES NOT HAVE A PRESENCE. THE PRELATURE FOCUSES ON EDUCATION, HEALTH AND THE ALLEVIATION OF POVERTY, AS WELL AS SPIRITUAL FORMATION.

TOP RIGHT Kimlea Girls' Technical training college has saved hundreds of girls from the exploitative child labour rampant on the coffee plantations in the Kianda region of Kenya.

CENTRE RIGHT Harambee 2002 continues centuries of Catholic missionary work, where the teaching of basic skills is thought as important as spiritual education.

BELOW Members of Opus Dei began Kimbondo, a social action programme on the outskirts of Kinshasa, in the Democratic Republic of the Congo, ten years ago in order to raise living standards for 12,000 people in the region, especially the women.

At first, dozens of Opus Dei members from other countries moved to the African continent to work as physicians, veterinarians, nurses, teachers and agricultural engineers. Now, there are 1,600 African-born members of Opus Dei who are continuing the work themselves.

It is one of the prelature's goals to encourage young Africans to promote the principles of ethics in politics and business in order to alleviate the corruption that has been a contributing factor to poverty and war across the continent.

One of the main Opus Dei ventures in Africa is Harambee 2002, founded to channel the prelature's gratitude for the canonization of Escrivá into practical social projects. In the last four years, Harambee, which is a Swahili word

meaning "working together", has financed 24 African-run projects in 14 African countries. The initiative focuses on Africans helping Africans, although Opus Dei centres around the world organize regular events to raise money to sponsor the project. Harambee has launched fund-raising campaigns to finance professional training programmes for women and young people who have fled from the fighting in southern Sudan and also for primary and secondary school faculties in Kenya. Money has also been raised to train artisans in Madagascar and to provide a health service programme for women and children in the Democratic Republic of the Congo.

CHARITY FOUNDATIONS

Opus Dei's corporate work in Africa includes individual charity foundations, part-funded by Harambee, such as the Kianda Foundation in Kenya. Kianda is a non-profit-making trust established in 1961 to provide education to women, and is now a household name in Kenya. Its managing director is co-founder María Angeles Canel, who was one of eight Opus Dei women sent to Kenya by Escrivá in 1961. Kianda has a school, a secretarial college, a technical training centre, small business training programmes, and teaches agriculture, health, home management, garment-making and machine knitting. It also has an outreach programme to help uneducated women in the surrounding villages, who work picking tea to support their families. Funding for the foundation is raised locally and internationally. In this region, only 75 per cent of the population has even a primary school-leaving qualification and 80 per cent of the adults are unemployed.

EDUCATION AND HEALTH

HIV and AIDS have ravaged Africa, with up to 700 people a day dying from the disease in Kenya alone. This leaves thousands of orphans and also elderly people without children to take care of them. Kimlea Girls Technical Training Centre, a part of the Kianda Foundation, is running a project to help women to understand the causes of AIDS. In a presentation to raise funds for the project, the foundation revealed that many village people in the area are unaware that the disease is transmitted sexually. They think that AIDS is a curse by an enemy or due to the anger of ancestors, and those who have it are often neglected by families, for fear of being similarly cursed.

Kimlea wants to help women to understand the causes of AIDS and how to care for sufferers. They offer healthcare and guidance via workshops and traditional means such as song, dance and drama. However, they are opposed to the use of

condoms, in line with the Catholic Church's prohibition of contraception, and instead encourage abstinence as a means of avoiding infection – an approach which has been criticized by members of the medical profession.

VIEWS OF LOCAL PEOPLE

The training and education given to women by Opus Dei centres in Africa focuses on basic home care and advice in small industries, which can be run from home. While international observers may wonder why the women are not educated to a higher standard and offered the opportunity to branch out into the wider world, the local people themselves welcome training that means they can stay at home, make a small income and become independent.

Women are often unable to spread their wings because of the African laws of inheritance, where a woman becomes the property of her dead husband's brother, and they may well be infected by AIDS, with children to take care of. In many cases, also, a husband will set out for work in a city, to make more money for his family, and never return. Local, simple work that will sustain the women and support their children is what they value, from making clothes to bee-keeping or animal husbandry.

ABOVE Monkole medical centre in Kinshasa, in the Democratic Republic of the Congo, offers healthcare to tens of thousands of people in situations of extreme need each year. The centre also provides programmes of physical hygiene and nutrition, home and neighbourhood sanitation, family health, child care and literacy.

ABOVE The red ribbon, the global symbol of solidarity with people who are HIV positive or are living with AIDS.

OPUS DEI IN THE FAR EAST

OPUS DEI MEMBERSHIP IS STILL LOW IN THE FAR EAST EXCEPT, PERHAPS, IN THE PHILIPPINES WHICH WAS ITS FIRST OUTPOST IN 1964, FOLLOWED BY HONG KONG IN 1981 AND SINGAPORE IN 1982. HOWEVER, ITS POPULARITY IS GROWING SWIFTLY. TODAY, THE PRELATURE ALSO HAS A PRESENCE IN TAIWAN AND SOME FOLLOWERS IN CHINA. ITS VIEWS ON THE SANCTITY OF WORK ARE GROWING STEADILY MORE POPULAR IN COUNTRIES WHERE WORK HAS BEEN REVERED FOR CENTURIES.

RIGHT Pupils from the Seido Mikawadai School in Nagasaki, Japan. Opus Dei's principle of following a founding father and promoting traditional family values is very popular with the Japanese, who have seen centuries-old traditions, which had been definitive guides for living and raising children, fragment.

BELOW An Asian family at Escrivá's canonization in Rome in 2002. The faithful travelled from 84 countries for the event: roughly one-third were Italian, another third were from the rest of Europe, and the rest were from the other continents.

At a Mass in Rome at the time of the canonization of Escrivá, the Bishop of Nagasaki, Takaaki Hirayama, talked of the excessive worry over work that is one of the greatest problems of the Japanese population, and how he thought that the message of sanctification of ordinary life could help alleviate such pressures as the technological age increased. Around 200 Opus Dei members from Hong Kong participated in another similar Mass in Rome, where Archbishop Joseph Ti-Kang of Taipei, in Taiwan, said that the value of work and the love towards the family espoused within Opus Dei are values rooted in Chinese culture. It was Opus Dei's office in Japan that asked the Sony Corporation to include a disclaimer in the film of *The Da Vinci Code*. It wanted the thriller

to be labelled as entirely fictional as "an expression of respect toward Jesus Christ, the history of the church and the religious beliefs of viewers".

RECOGNITION AND GRATITUDE

Opus Dei's popularity in the Philippines is demonstrated by the renaming of Amber Drive in the city of Pasig to Blessed Josemaría Escrivá Drive. The city made the change to express its gratitude for an Opus Dei-run university which it acknowledged had been a strong contributing factor in the economic boom and progress of the city since the 1970s. The University of Asia and the Pacific is a private university in the Philippines, which was formerly a centre of research and communications. Escrivá asked two of the first members of Opus Dei in the Philippines, Dr Jesus Estanislao and Dr Bernardo Villegas, to expand it into a university in the 1970s.

LEFT Dagatan was set up in 1988 with 35 students. By 2003, there were five more family farm schools in the Philippines, offering children of farmers the chance to alternate studies and field work and thus improve their earning capacity.

EDUCATIONAL PROJECTS

Three of Opus Dei's corporate works for education in the Far East are the Kam Him Centre in Hong Kong, the Dagatan Family Farm School and Anihan Technical School, both in the Philippines. Kam Him is based in Kowloon. In Cantonese, the word Kam means "tapestry", and Him means "modest". As well as organizing both secular and Christian activities for students of the area, the centre promotes social service projects for disadvantaged people.

Dagatan Family Farm School is one of five family farm schools in the Philippines, offering the children of farmers the possibility of alternative careers and field work to help their families improve their economic situation. Students go through a year-long cycle of one week in school and two weeks on their family's farm. Parents need to be willing to be actively involved in the teaching system of the school.

Anihan Technical School in Calamba City offers a two-year diploma course in food service for girls, with a speciality in baking. Opus Dei calls it "learning to bake with love". Along with culinary skills, students learn the principles of good business practice and entrepreneurship. Anihan also has an outreach project in one of the nearby neighbourhoods, where second year students teach children catechism, maths and personal hygiene.

LEFT Bobo Lee Yuen Chu, an insurance agent from Hong Kong, China, with her daughter. Bobo first heard about Opus Dei while at university. She has been a member ever since. She says that Josemaría's teachings are "an invitation to live by faith", and that "to try to reach holiness is easy: it involves doing your work well, conscientiously carrying out your duties and responsibilities while offering everything that you do to God".

REASONS FOR OPUS DEI'S POPULARITY

While Opus Dei always offers spiritual formation in all of its establishments and educational centres, it also aims to give the more disadvantaged end of society the opportunity for education and to learn how to build a business. Approximately three per cent of Hong Kong's seven million people are Catholic, the majority being Buddhist or Taoist, and Opus Dei's beliefs are not seen as any threat to the dominant faiths. In Japan, in particular, although the social structure has changed greatly since the end of the Second World War and the unquestioned divinity of the Emperor has ended, there is still a tendency towards identifying with the structure provided by a traditional and patriarchal organization such as Opus Dei, where the founder is revered and venerated.

PART FIVE

CONSPIRACY AND CRITICISM

 Opus Dei has been controversial within the Catholic Church and in the wider world since its inception in 1928. It has been accused of corruption, undue influence, secrecy, sado-masochism, fascism, brainwashing, being a cult, being anti-semitic, being part of the Freemasons, having surreptitious political, financial and religious influence in the world, being elitist, demeaning women and unethical recruiting. Escrivá's canonization in 2002 brought accusations of "fast-tracking", the financial "greasing of wheels", the suppression of evidence, and favouritism from Pope John Paul II. The prelature's membership of only 85,000 people worldwide serves to make the rumours more intense, as its members are all seen as influential.

RIGHT An estimated 300,000 pilgrims from around the world filled St Peter's Square in Rome during the canonization ceremony of Josemaría Escrivá, which took place on 6 October 2002.

THE DA VINCI CODE

DAN BROWN USED POPULAR MYTH AND LONG-ESTABLISHED THEOLOGICAL CONTROVERSIES IN HIS NOVEL *THE DA VINCI CODE*, MANY OF WHICH ARE SACRILEGE TO THE BELIEFS OF THE CATHOLIC CHURCH. THE BOOK CLAIMS THAT JESUS CHRIST MARRIED MARY MAGDALENE AND THAT THE LEGENDARY "HOLY GRAIL" IS NOT THE CUP THAT CHRIST USED AT THE LAST SUPPER BUT THE BLOODLINE FORGED BY THE CHILDREN OF JESUS AND MARY. THE CONCEPT THAT JESUS WAS CELIBATE THROUGHOUT HIS LIFE IS CENTRAL TO CATHOLIC THEOLOGY, AND THE HOLY GRAIL IS AN ARTHURIAN LEGEND THAT IS NOT PART OF CHRISTIAN DOCTRINE AT ALL.

RIGHT The Magdala Tower at Rennes Le Château, in the Languedoc region of France, was built by the mysterious priest Bérenger Saunière. The mystery of the Château is said to form the basis for much of Dan Brown's book *The Da Vinci Code*.

BELOW Leonardo Da Vinci's *The Last Supper* was completed in 1497 on a refectory wall of the church of Santa María delle Grazie, in Milan, Italy. The painting shows Jesus Christ seated with his twelve disciples at their last meal before his crucifixon.

The character of Mary Magdalene and the idea that she married Jesus and had his children is the most hotly debated aspect of *The Da Vinci Code*. To Catholics, and therefore to members of Opus Dei, the Bible is the foundation of all truth, and there is no mention in it of Jesus being married. To theologians, Mary Magdalene is a composite figure made up from various Biblical stories and often confused with a different woman, Mary of Bethany, sister of Lazarus. In the Gospel of Luke, Mary Magdalene is acknowledged as a follower of Jesus during his ministry, but in the other three Gospels, she only appears after the crucifixion. In the Catholic Church, the veneration of the Virgin Mary provides an altogether different,

but still powerful interpretation of the divine feminine. This aspect of faith is lacking in the Anglican Church, and it may be this loss of the idea of the divine feminine that has made *The Da Vinci Code* so popular. Unfortunately, there is no possibility of proving or disproving any of the theories about Jesus, Mary and a bloodline with any existing historical evidence. However, one theory is that such truths are hidden in the Vatican Library.

LINKS WITH OPUS DEI

The character most frequently associated with Opus Dei in *The Da Vinci Code* is Silas, an albino monk who commits murder in order to save the Catholic Church. However, the book has two characters who are members of Opus Dei: the second is Aringarosa, "Bishop of Opus Dei". Silas is in search of the Holy Grail, as is the hero of the book, Robert Langdon. However, Silas wants the information suppressed rather than revealed. He and the bishop hope that success in bringing the Grail to the evil Teacher may help to bring Opus Dei back into the Catholic Church's favour. Silas dies from gunshot wounds after accidentally shooting Bishop Aringarosa and escaping from police arrest.

Similarities in Silas's story to events in Opus Dei's history have linked this fictional character firmly with the group. Escrivá escaped from the Civil War in Spain via Andorra: Silas was imprisoned in Andorra after a life of crime. Like Escrivá, Silas practises severe corporal mortification, drawing blood. In the book, Dan Brown writes: "'Pain is good', Silas whispered, repeating the sacred mantra of Father Josemaría Escrivá — the teacher of all teachers. Although Escrivá had died in 1975, his wisdom lived on, his words still whispered by thousands of faithful

servants around the globe as they knelt on the floor and performed the sacred practice known as 'corporal mortification.'"

This quotation appears to reflect the truth of numeraries' lives. In *The Way*, Escrivá wrote: "Let us bless pain. Love pain, Sanctify pain ... Glorify pain!" (no. 208) However, it is an over-exaggeration of reality and, together with all other references to Opus Dei in the book, is fundamentally inaccurate.

ABOVE Catholic Filipino devotees engaging in self-flagellation as penitence for their sins, during the Lenten season in San Fernando. The Philippines is the only country in Asia with a predominantly Catholic population.

THE PILGRIMS FLOCK TO OPUS DEI IN LONDON

"Da Vinci Code Tours" have become big business for travel operators, with destinations including Paris, London, Rome and Scotland. Participants in the commercial tours in London visit the Temple Church in Fleet Street, Westminster Abbey and St James's Park. They are also told the location of Opus Dei's London office in Orme Court, although this, being more than three miles away from the main locations in the book, is too far for the official guided walks. However, groups of pilgrims can often be spotted standing in the street outside Orme Court.

LEFT Leonardo Da Vinci's *Mona Lisa* (c.1503–06). In his book, Dan Brown presents the painting as an androgynous self-portrait of the artist, intended to reflect the sacred union of male and female, implied in the holy union of Jesus and Mary Magdalene. Furthermore, "Mona Lisa" is an anagram for "Amon L'Isa", referring to the father and mother gods of ancient Egypt (Amon and Isis). This theory is universally rejected by art historians, who assert that the painting portrays a real woman, Lisa Gherardini, the wife of a Florentine cloth merchant, Francesco di Bartolomeo del Giocondo.

TRUTH OR FICTION

CONSPIRACY AND CRITICISM

THE LINE BETWEEN TRUTH AND FICTION IS OFTEN VERY NARROW. DAN BROWN, AUTHOR OF *THE DA VINCI CODE*, SAYS ON HIS OFFICIAL WEBSITE THAT HE IS CONFIDENT THAT HIS PORTRAYAL OF OPUS DEI IS ACCURATE. HE SAYS HIS SOURCES OF INFORMATION ARE BOOKS ABOUT THE PRELATURE — THE MAJORITY OF WHICH WERE WRITTEN BY HOSTILE EX-MEMBERS OF OPUS DEI — AND HIS OWN PERSONAL INTERVIEWS WITH CURRENT AND FORMER MEMBERS.

The only monks involved with Opus Dei are co-operators, and they live in their own order's monasteries. Another is that Silas's cilice cuts into his flesh — which is not how a cilice usually works, or how it is meant to work. Furthermore, Opus Dei is referred to as a sect, a Catholic Church, a congregation, a personal prelature of the pope himself, and a personal prelature of Vatican City. The word "personal" in personal prelature does not mean that Opus Dei is under the direct control of the pope or the Vatican, but that it is a non-geographical diocese.

ABOVE An 18th-century engraving of the Spanish Inquisition showing "flagellants and gentlemen". The Catholic Church has always focused on the suffering of Christ on the cross. It has seen the emulation of this suffering, to atone for sin, to be an important part of the development of self-discipline and spiritual strength.

RIGHT Dan Brown, author of *The Da Vinci Code*, who was unjustly accused of plagiarism in using the idea that Jesus and Mary Magdalene were married in his best-selling book.

In the "accredited facts" section of *The Da Vinci Code*, Brown writes: "The Vatican prelature known as Opus Dei is a deeply devout Catholic sect that has been the topic of recent controversy due to reports of brainwashing, coercion, and a dangerous practice known as 'corporal mortification'. Opus Dei has just completed construction of its $47 million National Headquarters at 243 Lexington Avenue in New York City."

WHAT ARE THE ERRORS?

It is a complicated exercise to point out the errors in *The Da Vinci Code*. One of the basic errors is that Opus Dei does not have monks as numeraries.

There are also totally unfounded accusations that Opus Dei members would kill for the sake of the Church and that Opus Dei entered a corrupt bargain with Pope John Paul II – bailing out the Vatican Bank in exchange for status as a personal prelature.

Dan Brown represents Opus Dei's centres as cloistered residence halls where people withdraw from the world to live a life of prayer. As British information officer, Jack Valero, comments: "It's not just that numeraries go out to work, it's that they are right in the middle of the world all the time. There is no difference between my living in Orme Court with other members and a friend of mine living with his wife and family. We both go out to work; we both come back home after work to eat, relax, sleep; we both watch the news and vote in elections; we both play sports and follow the World Cup; neither of us lives in a cell or spends the day in prayer!"

Dan Brown also refers to "brainwashing", "coercion", or "recruiting", with reference to Opus Dei, which are accusations that are common parlance on the Internet, but refuted by Opus Dei's information office. However, the reference in *The Da Vinci Code* to "the Bishop of Opus Dei" is technically correct: the prelate of Opus Dei, who is currently Father Javier Echevarría, is a consecrated bishop.

In *The Da Vinci Code*, Opus Dei members are depicted as murdering, lying, drugging people, and otherwise acting in a totally un-Christian way while thinking that it is justified for the sake of God, the Church or Opus Dei. The Opus Dei press office in the USA issued the following statement about *The Da Vinci Code*: "Opus Dei is a Catholic institution and adheres to Catholic doctrine, which clearly condemns immoral behaviour, including murder, lying, stealing, and generally injuring people. The Catholic Church teaches that one should never do evil, even for a good purpose."

For detractors, this has a hollow ring in light of many centuries of Catholic persecution of other religious groups, specifically the Spanish Inquisition of the 16th century. Although the Church has adapted to modern theological thought and teaches religious tolerance now, there are still pockets within it that do not accept these more contemporary interpretations; the same is true of other religious groups throughout the world.

ABOVE *The Da Vinci Code* highlights the incredible damage that would be done to the Catholic Church should Jesus be proved to have been a married man. The celibacy of Catholic priests is based on the belief in the celibacy of Christ and of St Paul.

BELOW Monks and nuns may be co-operators of the prelature, but full membership is denied to them. Silas, the monk in *The Da Vinci Code*, is a complete work of fiction.

CULTS

THE ENGLISH WORD "CULT" DERIVES FROM THE LATIN WORD *CULTUS* (CARE AND ADORATION). THE EARLIEST USE OF THE WORD IN A PURELY DEROGATORY SENSE IS BELIEVED TO HAVE BEEN IN WALTER MARTIN'S 1965 BOOK *THE KINGDOM OF THE CULTS*. FROM THE 1960S ONWARD, THE WORD "CULT" CAME TO DESCRIBE A SMALL, RELIGIOUS GROUP, OFTEN WITH A CHARISMATIC LEADER, WHICH ENGAGES IN BRAINWASHING AND OTHER MIND CONTROL TECHNIQUES AND IS PERCEIVED TO BE DANGEROUS. THE TERM IS ALSO USED WITHIN RELIGIONS TO DESCRIBE NEW CHARISMATIC MOVEMENTS. OPUS DEI HAS BEEN ACCUSED BY EX-MEMBERS OF BEING A CULT, WHICH IS STRONGLY DISPUTED BY THE PRELATURE.

ABOVE Sun Myung Moon performs a group wedding ceremony in New York for some 22,000 couples. Some sociologists and scholars of new religious movements have written that Moon's leadership of the Unification Church is based on charismatic authority.

RIGHT The burning of the Mount Carmel Centre ranch headquarters of the Branch Davidians, following an FBI siege. Vernon Howell, head of the cult, legally changed his name to David Koresh, in the belief that he was head of the biblical house of David, from which Judeo-Christian tradition maintains the Messiah will come.

Leo Pfeffer, who was the leading theoretician on the separation of church and state in the USA until his death in 1993, summed up the difference between a religion, a sect and a cult in the following way: "If you believe in it, it is a religion or perhaps 'the' religion; and if you do not care one way or another about it, it is a sect; but if you fear and hate it, it is a cult." Opus Dei has often been referred to by its critics as a cult.

IS OPUS DEI A CULT?

Roman Catholicism uses the Latin word *cultus* as a technical term for the veneration extended to a particular saint. Given their allegiance to their founder, under its own church's definition, Opus Dei could, indeed, be defined as a cult.

Professor Margaret Thaler Singer, author of *Cults in Our Midst*, writes that religious groups and altruistic movements are often mistaken for cults. The main difference is that these groups and movements are focused outward, attempting to better the lives of members and non-members or making altruistic contributions to the world. Cults serve their own purposes, which are the purposes of the cult leader, and their energies are focused inward rather than outward. This definition confirms that Opus Dei is not a cult.

Jeffrey Hadden PhD, a Teaching Technology Fellow at the University of Virginia, who runs the Religious Movements Homepage project at the university, believes that cults are most often in the eye of the already angry beholder. He writes: "Much of the mischief of the popular meaning

of the word 'cult' results from the organized efforts of disgruntled former members. These anti-cultists are joined by parents who blame 'cults' for the decisions of their (usually) adult children to join groups that did not meet with their approval."

RECRUITMENT TECHNIQUES

Social psychologist, Kelton Rhoads, PhD, a specialist in the study of "influence", suggests that the condition that makes people much more open to joining a group that others might consider a cult is loneliness. This could be caused by moving to a new country, leaving the parental home or the ending of a relationship. At such times, being welcomed into a group is much appreciated. Once the friendship is established and the beliefs of the "cult" are revealed, it will either appeal or repulse. Another factor in successful recruitment for a cult is the perception that it is "God's elect" and the only way to become pure where all others are defiled.

In the case of Opus Dei, their education centres, training colleges and hostels provide ideal places for people to find structure and friendship and Escrivá's own injunctions to proselytize are

quoted across the Internet. In Opus Dei's journal *Crónica* in 1971, he wrote: "Go out to the highways and byways and push those whom you find to come and fill my house, force them to come in; push them." There are also several personal accounts from ex-members of Opus Dei accusing the prelature of coercion, and it is obvious from the anger of vociferous ex-members that they either did not understand the rules of membership, or that they were not given correct information when they did join.

However, each centre is under the control of a different director and has a different character. Some Opus Dei members may overstepped the mark, and their actions have hurt people badly, but others have behaved with courtesy and decorum. It is also worth noting that levels of membership in Opus Dei are growing very slowly indeed, at approximately 650 per year. If they are trying to recruit as avidly as their founder wished them to do, then their tactics are not working.

LEFT François-Marie Arouet, better known as the French writer and philosopher Voltaire, is the best-known historical opposer of cults. Voltaire professed deism and a rational approach to religion, rejecting rituals, supernaturalism, superstitions and formal cults as curtailing people's freedom.

BELOW St Josemaría Escrivá was almost fanatically devoted to his calling and did not care if his zeal was misinterpreted. The note in his handwriting below reads: "Misunderstood? Perhaps, if your cross is to achieve its full significance, you need to live like this, without being understood. Another generation will understand you."

¿Yncomprensión? —duiza, para que tu cruz tenga to do su relieve, hace falta que vivas así, sin que te comprendan. Otra generación te entenderá.

FAMOUS CULTS
The best-known cult is the Moonies – members of Reverend Sun Myung Moon's Unification Church, where thousands of participants marry strangers in the same movement in simultaneous marriages. More tragic examples include the People's Temple in Jonestown, Guyana, where more than 900 followers of the Rev. Jim Jones committed suicide in 1978, and the Movement for the Restoration of the Ten Commandments, in Uganda, where up to 1,000 members died in what was assumed to be a mass suicide. They were a breakaway group from the Catholic Church, and believed that the end of the world was coming. Other cults involved in suicides include the Solar Temple, Heaven's Gate and the Students of the Seven Seals. The latter was involved in tragedy at Waco, Texas, in 1993, when David Koresh and more than 70 of his followers (often known as Branch Davidians) died.

OPUS DEI AND SECRECY

As far back as the 1930s, Opus Dei has had a reputation for secrecy. It was referred to as the White Masons because people believed that members worshipped in rooms filled with masonic and mystical symbols. At one point they were also thought to follow the ancient traditions of the Kabbalah. In 1941, a well-respected and influential Jesuit priest, Father Ángel Carrillo de Albornóz, publicly accused them of being a secretive and heretical society influenced by Freemasonry.

RIGHT Italian Giovanni Trapattoni, former coach of Italy's national soccer team, says that Escrivá "teaches athletes that their efforts in training and in competition, their esteem for opponents, their humility in victory and good spirit in defeat, are a path for reaching God and serving others".

BELOW An illustration of the interior of a Masonic Temple. The two pillars represent the power and might of God; the sun represents wisdom and is a reminder to strive for intellectual expansion.

In the 1930s, rumours of links between Opus Dei and Freemasonry became so prevalent that a civil court known as the Tribunal for the Repression of Masonry investigated the allegations. They found no truth in them but both the government of Spain and the police continued investigations on and off for another five years. In the book *Conversations with Monsignor Escrivá*, the founder of Opus Dei is quoted as saying: "The members of The Work detest secrecy because they are ordinary faithful, the same as anyone else. It would be repulsive for them to carry a sign on their back that said: 'Let it be known that I am dedicated to the service of God.'"

THE "SECRET" CONSTITUTION

Opus Dei has no secret constitution. What it does have is a set of statutes written in Latin, which very few people can understand. The statutes are the law that governs Opus Dei, as approved by the Vatican. The original constitution of 1950 was superseded in 1982, when the statutes were approved by the Holy See.

The original constitution was not believed to represent Opus Dei accurately, being a compromise between what Escrivá wanted and what the Church would then allow. Escrivá was

never happy with this compromise and was reluctant for the constitution to become too public until suitable changes were made.

The statutes can now be read, in translation, on the Opus Dei Awareness Network website. They mostly consist of details of the structure of Opus Dei: how people should live and the prelature's duties towards members. They also include descriptions of what is expected of candidates and state that people unhappy in The Work should be encouraged to leave of their own free will, and that if dismissal is necessary, it should be done "with the greatest charity".

SECRECY IN THE WORKPLACE
Opus Dei members are not deliberately secretive. Just like Buddhists, Jews, Hindus, Muslims and other Christians, Opus Dei members do not necessarily pronounce their faith in public. A member of Opus Dei may have a crucifix or a picture of the Virgin Mary on his or her desk, but that just points to Christianity.

In the same way, Opus Dei centres are called by simple names such as Ashwell House, Netherhall or Grandpont; they do not have a plaque outside saying Opus Dei. However, if the house or organization has a website, then there will either be an open acknowledgement of inspiration or

a connection with Opus Dei, or there will be a link to Opus Dei's own site in the links page. Opus Dei people will base their decisions at work or home on their religious belief, therefore this will influence any business in which they have authority. This is only a problem if it is to be believed that Opus Dei has a specific brief to infiltrate and evangelize.

Robert Hutchison, author of *Their Kingdom Come: Inside the Secret World of Opus Dei*, came up with the name "Octopus Dei" to describe the power that the prelature's members have through their individual connections in education, the media, publishing and film production. For example, Jan Michelini, director's assistant to Mel Gibson on the multi-million-dollar-taking film *The Passion*, is a supernumerary. Jan was baptized by the Pope at the beginning of John Paul II's papacy, and he was present at a preview showing of *The Passion* to the Pope. After this, the rumour spread that John Paul II had approved the film and that was why it became an overnight success. However, Mel Gibson showed the film in private screenings to evangelical churches across the USA, which would have had just as great an effect. The Opus Dei connection also led to rumours that *The Passion* is an Opus Dei movie, and that its producer is a member of the prelature. Mel Gibson is *not* a member of Opus Dei, and neither was anyone else in the film's production or finance team.

LEFT Vatican spokesman Joaquín Navarro-Valls delivering a medical bulletin on Pope John Paul II's failing health. The Vatican is no stranger to accusations of conspiracy, and its strong stance on celibacy and against homosexuality make accusations of sexual abuse against Catholic priests even more damaging for the Church.

BELOW Opus Dei's statutes are written in Latin, which makes them unintelligible to the majority of people.

OPUS DEI PEOPLE OF INFLUENCE
Out of 85,000 members, approximately 100 could be judged as being influential. Powerful members, past and present, include: Joaquín Navarro-Valls, head of the Vatican press office and former head of the Foreign Press Association in Rome; Luis Valls, former executive chairman of Banco Popular in Spain; Ruth Kelly, Community and Local Government Secretary, United Kingdom; Archbishop Justo Mullor, president of the Accademia Ecclesiastica school for Vatican diplomats; Cardinal Juan Luis Cipriani Thorne, Archbishop of Lima; and Cardinal Julián Herranz Casado, President of Interpretation of Legislative Texts for the Roman Curia. Giovanni Trapattoni, former coach for the Italian national football team, is a keen supporter of Opus Dei.

OBJECTIONS TO OPUS DEI

THERE ARE MANY, MOSTLY UNFOUNDED ACCUSATIONS OF FASCISM, ANTI-SEMITISM AND MISOGYNY AGAINST OPUS DEI — THE MOST CONVINCING AND TELLING ONES COMING FROM THOSE PEOPLE WHO WERE ONCE MEMBERS OF THE PRELATURE. THE MOST SENSATIONAL OF THE ACCUSATIONS AGAINST OPUS DEI ARE LEVELLED AT ESCRIVÁ. REV. IAN PAISLEY'S EUROPEAN INSTITUTE OF PROTESTANT STUDIES WEBSITE EVEN ACCUSES HIM OF BEING THE PRIVATE CONFESSOR TO GENERAL FRANCO. THE WEBSITE ALSO CLAIMS THAT HE WAS SPIRITUAL ADVISOR TO GENERAL AUGUSTO PINOCHET. NEITHER OF THESE CLAIMS HAS ANY FOUNDATION WHATSOEVER, BUT THEY FUEL THE FIRES OF CONTROVERSY AROUND OPUS DEI.

ABOVE Bishop Álvaro del Portillo meets Pope John Paul II at the canonization of Josemaría Escrivá. An estimated 300,000 pilgrims from around the world attended the canonization ceremony.

María del Carmen Tapia, who worked in the Opus Dei secretariat in Rome and wrote *Beyond the Threshold: A Life in Opus Dei,* realized that she herself became a fanatic while she was in Opus Dei. She came to believe that the approval of Escrivá was the only way to please God. Tapia became the centre of a storm of controversy when she was not called to give evidence for Escrivá's beatification and over accusations that Opus Dei made about her behaviour while still a member.

Professor Denys Turner, a lecturer in theology at Cambridge University, was a member for eight years in the 1960s. He acknowledges that Opus Dei may have changed since then but says he was aware of a kind of mind control going on. For him, leaving was "a catastrophic experience"; he was told that he would "lose his soul".

OPUS DEI AWARENESS NETWORK

Tammy DiNicola, an ex-numerary, and her mother, Dianne, founded the Opus Dei Awareness Network (ODAN) in 1990. Tammy's decision to leave after three years came with "exit counselling" with external advisors who were working with evidence from ex-numerary, Dr John Roche. Both DiNicola and Roche have specialized in writing and speaking about the prelature ever since, attracting evidence from other ex-members who are also committed to expressing their anger over their treatment.

Dr Roche has written many published articles about Opus Dei, particularly on the prelature's attitudes to recruiting and leaving. In *The Clergy Review* in 1985, he wrote: "In 1972, a Spanish numerary boasted to me that 60 boys had joined The Work in one club in Bilbao, Spain in that year alone ... Opus Dei commonly engineers the crisis of vocation during a summer course where a group of 'well-formed' young people are isolated from outside contacts for several weeks, supervised constantly, and subjected to a sustained pressure to join The Work. They are never left to themselves, and visitors or outside visits are not allowed."

In 2006, ODAN joined forces with the Brazilian group Opus Livre (www.opuslivre.org) and the Spanish Opus Libros (www.opuslibros.org) to form the International Collaboration for Truth about Opus Dei (ICTOD).

OBJECTIONS TO CANONIZATION

Escrivá died in 1975 and was canonized in 2002. Allegations flew that this was the fastest-ever canonization, and that Opus Dei had manipulated the process. The former is demonstrably untrue, and the latter is refuted both by Opus Dei and the Vatican. Cardinal Angelo Felici and Archbishop Edward Nowak of the Congregation for the Causes of Saints in 1992 issued a statement on Escrivá's beatification saying: "Opposition has been expressed and this was foreseeable, given the spread of Opus Dei's members and of the work they do in service to the Church. There were also some insinuations about the procedure followed in this specific case by the Congregation for the Causes of Saints. These insinuations are completely groundless." The statement adds: "After the Servant of God's death in Rome on 26 June 1975, the reputation for sanctity which he enjoyed while living became increasingly widespread. Over the next five years the postulation was able to collect, in two volumes of 428 and 390 pages, many testimonies about the basis and extent of this reputation."

Other objections included the fact that many of those who publicly opposed Escrivá's canonization were not called to give "Devil's Advocate" witness. ODAN claims that the surgeon who headed the medical board that reviews potential miracles was an Opus Dei member. Opus Dei denies that Dr Raffaello-Cortesini was involved in any way in Escrivá's cause.

CRUEL TREATMENT

Physically, the only abuse within Opus Dei appears to have been self-inflicted. Emotionally, the toll from misunderstandings, lack of knowledge, emotional and spiritual coercion and blackmail, whether real or perceived, has been great among a small minority.

In her book *El Opus Dei: Anexo a una Historia*, María Angustias Moreno wrote: "To leave The Work is a great disgrace ... the founder asserted that he would not give five cents for the soul of one who left ... If any member of The Work shows interest [in someone who has left] the reply of the directors is 'those who have left are as if dead.'" Opus Dei representatives are at pains to point out that this is not the approach taken to ex-members nowadays. Dr Roche testifies that there has been enormous pain to families whose children were not allowed to freely visit their parents. Existing numeraries in the UK counter this by saying that they are on excellent terms with their families.

ABOVE Worshippers at the Mass of Thanksgiving for the canonization of St Josemaría Escrivá in Rome on 10 October 2002. During 8–10 October, 29 Masses of Thanksgiving were said in Rome in 17 different languages. The relics of Josemaría were finally taken back to their usual location in the prelatic Church of Our Lady of Peace in Rome.

LEFT St Josemaría Escrivá was accused of over-coercion, temper and self-flagellation, but his commitment to his beliefs has never been questioned.

LESSONS LEARNED

THE MORE PUBLICITY THAT OPUS DEI RECEIVES, THE MORE IT MUST REALIZE THAT DIFFERENT CENTRES OPERATE IN DIFFERENT WAYS AND THAT TRANSPARENCY AND CONSISTENCY ARE ITS BEST FRIENDS. THE MAJORITY OF ANGER FROM EX-MEMBERS COMES FROM THOSE WHO LEFT 15 OR MORE YEARS AGO, SO IT IS HOPED THAT THE SITUATION IS IMPROVING. HOWEVER, THERE ARE STILL REPORTS — MOSTLY IN CHAT-ROOMS ON THE INTERNET — OF "OVER-RECRUITING", IN WHICH PEOPLE ARE SUSPICIOUS AND REPELLED BY THE APPROACHES OF SOME OPUS DEI MEMBERS.

RIGHT Bishop Echevarría comments on an Italian newspaper containing an interview on the film of *The Da Vinci Code*, before its premiere at Cannes in 2006. He has said some good might come out of the film. He admits to having thumbed through the book but has commented, "I don't have time to waste on little novels for the naive."

BELOW *The Forge* is Josemaría's Escrivá's last book, and it was written as a collection of points for meditation. *In Love with the Church* is a collection of four homilies by Escrivá. Twelve editions have been published in nine languages since 1986.

Many members of Opus Dei have been deeply hurt by the criticisms levelled at them and the fact that past problems with ex-members have been catapulted into the limelight afresh by *The Da Vinci Code*. However, as time goes on and they accept that the attention will not die down for some years, they are recognizing that strong reaction and anger serve no purpose at all.

What is required of Opus Dei is a more open public face. Opus Dei is attempting to embrace the media-hungry world of disclosure, no matter how uncomfortable it may seem to them at times. While it emphasizes that the lives of its individual members are their business, it has accepted that the public wishes to know about it and has come out of the shadows to tell all that it can.

INCREASED OPENNESS

The membership would be foolish not to capitalize on the wider knowledge of their existence in order to spread the word about their mission. When John Allen wrote *Opus Dei: Secrets and Power inside the Catholic Church*, in 2004, Opus Dei allowed him unprecedented access to its people and information, and it continues to open up to press and public scrutiny. However, Opus

a canonized saint. For Opus Dei members, obedience to superiors is mandatory; women are better at home-making than men; there should be celibacy for priests, and no female priests; Mass must be attended every day and confession made regularly. They believe that it is a holy duty to teach and guide people and attract them to the Church and, if possible, to Opus Dei itself.

For the secular world of the 21st century, all these views are verging on the unacceptable. However, the current spread of Christian evangelism and Islam demonstrate that concepts of religious purity and fundamentalism are still strong among a certain sector of the population.

LEFT Leo Maliksi, a Filipino national and a numerary of Opus Dei, shows his cilice to clarify the misconstruction from the film *The Da Vinci Code,* during a meeting of the Chinese Regional Bishops' Conference in Taiwan, in May 2006. Maliksi states there are 17 Opus Dei numeraries in Taiwan who wear the cilice on the leg for two hours a day to execute corporal mortification.

BELOW John Allen, the Vatican correspondent for the *National Catholic Reporter*, at a press conference to discuss his book on Opus Dei.

Dei will never be able to lay formalized accounts on the table for an interested press or to state how many supernumeraries are married to non-Christian partners or what percentage of members leave each year, for the simple reason that they do not know. Each centre is its own family, as is each country. They are as discreet with each other as they have been with the world.

ACKNOWLEDGING MISTAKES

Opus Dei members know that serious mistakes have been made with respect to recruiting and the treatment of some members, and that it is important to acknowledge that.

In December 2004, Bishop Javier Echevarría, prelate of Opus Dei, made the following statement to John Allen for his book: "I say this with all sincerity and from the bottom of my heart. If we have hurt anyone; if we have failed anyone, we ask their forgiveness."

POLITICAL CORRECTNESS

Opus Dei is not, and never will be, politically correct. It believes that the lore of the Catholic Church is fundamental truth. These restrictions are seen through the eyes of their founder,

"NO PUBLICITY IS BAD PUBLICITY"

"There's no such thing as bad publicity except your own obituary." The well-known saying from Irish author and dramatist Brendan Behan is proving to be true for Opus Dei. For every salacious rumour and every accusation there is also another person who, for the first time, hears about the prelature and may be interested in joining it. Escrivá's books, instead of being printed and published by small academic presses, are now hot property. What had been a group only publicized by an underground movement of criticism, discounted by most people, is now big news.

INFORMING THE PUBLIC

OPUS DEI IS NEWS. NEVER, SINCE ITS FOUNDING, HAVE MORE PEOPLE IN THE WORLD KNOWN ABOUT IT — AND THE PRELATURE WAS QUICK TO USE THE PUBLICITY FROM DAN BROWN'S *THE DA VINCI CODE* IN A WORLDWIDE PUBLICITY CAMPAIGN. IN AN ERA OF POLITICAL SPIN, THEY REALIZED THAT DENIAL AND SECRECY WOULD ONLY FUEL THE FIRES AGAINST THEM. NOT ONCE HAS OPUS DEI SPOKEN OUT IN ANGER AT ACCUSATIONS AGAINST THE PRELATURE. THEY HAVE OFFERED THE MEDIA ACCESS TO THEIR MEMBERS AND CENTRES — BUT HAVE STILL KEPT CONTROL OF WHO SPEAKS AND WHEN.

ABOVE Pope Benedict XVI is presented with a piano-shaped cake for his birthday, which is on 16 April, during an audience with young members of Opus Dei, in the Paul VI hall of the Vatican, 10 April 2006.

In the spring of 2006, Opus Dei launched a comprehensive, updated website including links to Escrivá's own site. The main site, www.opusdei.org, has satellite sites for different countries. Just before the opening of the film *The Da Vinci Code*, the site posted an open letter to the Sony corporation concerning the film, including this section: "In recent months, it is possible that you may have heard about Opus Dei, in the context of the aforementioned film. It is likely that for many, this was the first time that you have had occasion to hear the name of this institution of the Church, and some of you might have wished to know more about it. Therefore, this office feels obliged to state its availability to inform whoever wants to know about the real Opus Dei, which has nothing to do with the description sketched in the novel. Whoever wants information can ask this office, and we will respond as soon as possible with great pleasure: our doors are wide open."

The letter also appeals to the corporation to consider that the book on which the film is based, revolves around the idea that the Christian faith is founded on a lie, and that the Catholic Church has over the centuries employed criminal and violent means to keep people in ignorance. It states that the Church does not deserve this kind of disrespect. The site contains information about the canonization of Escrivá, conferences and events around the world, and refutations of many of the allegations against Escrivá and the prelature itself. It also contains information on joining Opus Dei.

WEBSITES, BOOKS AND EVENTS

Apart from the Opus Dei Awareness Network, which is regularly maintained by the DiNicolas, who are also regular guests on American news programmes, the most prominent unofficial website is called just that: *Opus Dei: the Unofficial Website*. The site is run by Franz Schäfer who claims that it is not meant as anti-Opus Dei propaganda, "but as Opus Dei itself only present themselves in a good light, there is an emphasis on critical points of view". Opus Dei also features on the Nick A. Ross Institute for the Study of Destructive Cults, Controversial Groups and Movements website (www.nickross.com) and on many other sites that investigate religious groups.

The Way, Escrivá's first book of sayings, has been published, and a month before the launch of the film *The Da Vinci Code*, a new DVD showing "The real Opus Dei" was released by the St Josemaría Institute. The DVD *Passionately Loving the World* features members and co-operators talking about their lives and connection both to Opus Dei and to its founder.

VIEWS OF FRIENDLY EX-MEMBERS

If you type the words "Opus Dei" into an Internet search engine, it will reveal that there are many ex-members of Opus Dei who have no axe to grind with the prelature. The most prominent on the Internet is Matthew G. Collins, who manages the "Trust the Truth" blog: www.interbit.com/blogger/OpusDeiFAQ.html. Matthew introduces himself in this way: "I'm happily married with three children, live in Baltimore, MD and work at a hospital in Baltimore as a computer programmer. I was a supernumerary member of Opus Dei for almost 27 years. I left Opus Dei on my own initiative for personal reasons, but remain friendly toward the organization, and am now a co-operator. The FAQ was originally written while I was still a member but I have not changed any of the substance it contains since I left, and have no reason to do so." Matthew's site offers probably the most easily understandable and clearest outline of Opus Dei on the web. It is written from a devoutly Catholic point of view, but does not skip any of the controversial issues. In answer to a question on whether Opus Dei forbids birth control, he says: "No. God does."

LEFT Pope Benedict XVI, at the bottom of the picture in white, blesses the statue of Josemaría Escrivá, placed in a niche of the outside wall of St Peter's Basilica. The blessing took place in September 2005, at the end of the weekly general audience at the Vatican.

CONCLUSION

There is one word that sums up Opus Dei better than any other and that word is "family". The members of Opus Dei belong to a worldwide family of friends and fellow believers, all of whom have the same beliefs, standards and goals. Every one of them is committed to practising orthodox Catholicism; every one of them venerates Escrivá. But like all families, there are black sheep, skeletons in the cupboard and a deep, subconscious belief that *their* family is more important than any other.

The Roman Catholic Church teaches adherents that Catholicism is the only true faith, and the evidence of centuries of religious warfare demonstrates that there is always danger where there is fanaticism. In the case of Opus Dei, the prelature's swift and efficient grasp of the 21st-century world of spin and marketing, once they were highlighted by unrequested publicity, is as unsettling as it is impressive.

ABOVE A saintly image of Josemaría, displayed on prayer cards that were distributed to the public at his canonization in 2002. His feast day is celebrated on 26 June.

GLOSSARY

Assistant numeraries
Women who perform all the domestic duties for men and for women at Opus Dei centres. They receive the same spiritual formation as numeraries and associates, make the Fidelity and practise self-mortification.

Associates
Members who live a celibate life and follow the most rigorous spiritual practices in Opus Dei, but who, for work or family reasons, do not live in an Opus Dei centre. They make the Fidelity and practise self-mortification.

Beatification
The first official stage on the pathway to sainthood. Except in the case of a martyr, it must be proved that one healing miracle has occurred after believers have prayed to the potential saint to intercede for them. The candidate is then known as "blessed".

Canonization
The final stage to becoming a saint. A further miracle must be demonstrated and a study carried out into the life of the candidate. Once conferred, sainthood is irrevocable.

Cardinal
A cardinal is a senior official in the Catholic Church ranking just below the pope. Each is appointed personally by the pope. They lead their own dioceses and archdioceses or run sections of the Vatican. Popes are elected by the votes of the cardinals.

Catholic Church
The name used by the branch of the Christian Church that dates directly back to the 1st century. It later divided into many different Christian denominations. Also referred to as the Roman Catholic Church. The head of the Catholic Church is the pope.

Cilice
A spiked chain that assistant numeraries, numeraries and associates wear on their upper thigh for two hours a day as an act of self-mortification.

Co-operators
People who are not members of Opus Dei, but who support the prelature with prayer, volunteer work or financial contributions.

Corporate work
An educational, medical or social venture run by Opus Dei members (often with other people), which has Opus Dei board members and follows Opus Dei spiritual teachings. It is not a venture owned by Opus Dei.

Da Vinci Code (The)
The best-selling novel by Dan Brown featuring two fictional characters who are members of Opus Dei.

Devil's advocate
The devil's advocate was a canon lawyer appointed by the Church to argue against the virtues of a proposed candidate for sainthood. He was employed to look for flaws in the evidence of miracles and good works. The office was established in 1587 but was abolished by Pope John Paul II in 1983.

Diocese
An administrative territorial area governed by a bishop, also referred to as an episcopal see. A more important area is known as an archdiocese (due to its large size or historical significance, or both) and is governed by an archbishop.

Discipline
A knotted cord used like a whip which associates, assistant numeraries and numeraries of Opus Dei use approximately once a week to flagellate themselves while saying a short vocal prayer.

Ecumenical
Of or relating to the worldwide Christian church. An ecumenical council therefore is a council debating issues that concern the Church worldwide.

Epiphany
A festival of the Christian church, held on 6 January, celebrating the coming of the Magi (the Three Wise Men) to Bethlehem with gifts for the infant Jesus, and symbolizing the manifestation of Jesus to the world. It is the 12th day after Christmas, and marks the end of the Christmas festivities.

Fidelity
The process of pledging a lifetime's commitment to Opus Dei. Fidelity is pledged after five years for numeraries, associates and assistant numeraries but can be pledged any time or not at all by supernumeraries.

Formation
This is the word used for the shaping and moulding of a specific belief system into a deep and abiding faith. Christian spiritual formation is intended to help believers become more fully united with Christ. It is increasingly popular in evangelical Christian churches.

Holy See
The diocese of the pope.

Immaculate Conception
The dogma of Immaculate Conception is that the soul of the Virgin Mary was conceived without the stigma of original sin and that she lived an earthly life completely free from sin.

Martyr

Someone who dies for their faith.

Mass

One of the seven Sacraments, Mass is the central act of Catholic worship and a celebration of the Last Supper, Jesus' last meal with his disciples, with wine representing his blood and bread representing his body.

Norms

The spiritual practices that Opus Dei members perform every day, including reciting the Rosary, going to Mass and saying specific prayers.

Numeraries

People who give a lifetime of celibacy to Opus Dei. They live in Opus Dei centres but work in the outside world. They do not make vows, but after five years at the prelature they make the Fidelity.

Opus Dei

Latin for "the work of God", Opus Dei describes the life of commitment of some orders of monks and nuns, as well as being the name of the personal prelature founded by St Josemaría Escrivá.

Personal prelature

A personal prelature is made up from a prelate (generally a bishop), clergy and often the laity, all working together to meet specific needs of the Church. It is named a "personal" prelature to distinguish it from a "territorial" prelature, because the limits of its jurisdiction are defined by the members – who may live in different countries – and not by geographical boundaries. Opus Dei is the first personal prelature in the Catholic Church.

Prelate

A prelate is generally a bishop: a member of the clergy who either has ordinary jurisdiction over a group of people or ranks in precedence with ordinaries.

Pope

The pope is the leader of the Catholic Church. He is elected by a College of Cardinals who meet, behind closed doors, in the Sistine Chapel, in Rome. The office is for life.

Rosary

A traditional form of Catholic devotion involving a string of prayer beads with a crucifix and a litany of set prayers.

Sacraments

Catholic life is defined by the seven Sacraments, which are referred to as an outward and visible sign of God's inner, invisible grace. They are: baptism, confession, Holy Eucharist (Mass or communion), confirmation, marriage, ordination and extreme unction (the anointing of the sick, or last rites).

Saint

A Catholic person who has been judged, after their death, to have lived a life of exemplary virtue, and through whose intercession, healing has been received. The two stages of achieving sainthood are beatification and canonization.

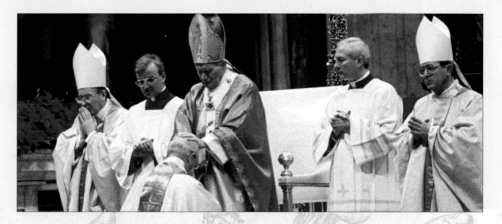

Self-mortification

The practice of self-denial and, occasionally, inflicting discomfort or even pain on the physical body. The Catholic Church believes that self-mortification has great spiritual value, especially in helping people to resist temptations that lead to sin.

Spanish Inquisition

The Spanish Inquisition was part of the Holy Inquisition, originally set up by Pope Gregory IX in 1232 to seek out and destroy heresy within the Church.

The Spanish Inquisition was set up by King Ferdinand and Queen Isabella of Spain in 1478 under Inquisitor-General Tomás Torquemada. It was at its height until 1492, when all Jews were expelled

from Spain. Up to 2,000 people died in 14 years. The Spanish Inquisition continued up to about 1700, with nearly 1,000 further deaths. It was ended after the Napoleonic Wars in 1835. However, the Holy Inquisition continued until 1908, when it was given the name Holy Office, and in 1965 it was renamed Congregation for the Doctrine of the Faith.

Supernumeraries

Members who are not celibate, and who live in their own homes, but who are committed to Opus Dei. They are often married couples. They may also make the Fidelity.

The Work

What Opus Dei members call their life of spiritual sanctification of work. It is a short form of Opus Dei – "the work of God".

Vatican

The Vatican is the smallest independent nation state in the world, situated in Rome. It is the home of the government of the Catholic Church, whose leader is the pope.

Vocation

The "call from God" to give one's life to holy work, whether as a cleric, a monk or nun, or a layperson. A vocation will generally include a commitment for life to some religious or spiritual organization.

Whistling

The process of applying for membership of Opus Dei. It is a reference to the whistling of an old-fashioned kettle when it has started to boil after a long period of heating up.

INDEX

94

INDEX

BIBLIOGRAPHY

Allen, John

Opus Dei: The Truth about its Rituals, Secrets and Power (UK paperbacks – with several different titles) (Penguin 2006)

Berglar, Peter

Opus Dei: Life and Work of Its Founder Josemaría Escrivá (Scepter 1995)

Bernal, Salvador

Alvaro Del Portillo: Bishop Prelate of Opus Dei (Four Courts Press 1999)

Coverdale, John

Uncommon Faith: The Early Years of Opus Dei, 1928–1943 (Four Courts Press 2002)

Del Carmen Tapia, Maria

Beyond the Threshold: A Life in Opus Dei (Continuum International Publishing Group 1998)

Escrivá de Balaguer, Josemaría

The Way (Image 2006)

Conversations with Josemaría Escrivá de Balaguer (Scepter 2003)

Friedlander, Noam

What is Opus Dei? (Collins & Brown 2005)

Hahn, Scott

Ordinary Work, Extraordinary Grace: My Spiritual Journey in Opus Dei (Doubleday 2006)

Hutchison, Robert

Their Kingdom Come: Inside the Secret World of Opus Dei (Corgi 2005)

Keenan, William

St Josemaría Escrivá and the Origins of Opus Dei (Gracewing 2004)

Le Tourneau, Dominique

What is Opus Dei? (Gracewing 2002)

Messori, Vittorio

Opus Dei: Leadership and Vision in Today's Catholic Church (Regnery Publishing Inc 1997)

Ocáriz, Fernando

The Canonical Path of Opus Dei (Scepter 1994)

Opus Dei

Opus Dei and The Da Vinci Code (DVD) (Bfs Entertainment 2006)

Reese, Thomas J

Inside the Vatican: Politics and Organization of the Catholic Church (Harvard University Press 1996)

Rodriguez, Pedro, Ocáriz, Fernando and Illanes, José Luis

Opus Dei in the Church: An Ecclesiological Study of the Life and Apostolate of Opus Dei (Scepter 2003)

Romano, Giuseppe (translated by Edmund C Lane)

Opus Dei: Who, How, Why (Alba House 1995)

Vázquez de Prada, Andrés

The Founder of Opus Dei: Volume I, The Life of Josemaría Escrivá, The Early Years (Scepter 2000)

The Founder of Opus Dei: The Divine Ways on Earth: Volume II, God and Daring. (Scepter 2003)

The Founder of Opus Dei: Volume III, The Divine Ways on Earth (Scepter 2003)

Walsh, Michael J

Opus Dei: An Investigation into the Powerful, Secretive Society within the Catholic Church (HarperSanFrancisco 2004)

Walsh, Michael J

The Secret World of Opus Dei (Grafton Books 1990)